POSITIVE STORIES FOR THE CURIOUS SOUL

A COLLECTION OF UPLIFTING & FEEL-GOOD STORIES TO BRING YOU HAPPINESS, JOY AND LAUGHTER

CHARLIE MILLER

ISBN: 978-1-64845-129-4

CONTENTS

CONTENTS

INTRODUCTION

*"They say a person needs just three things to truly be happy in this world: someone to **love**, something to **do**, and something to **hope for**."*
– Tom Bodett, writer and other things.

Welcome to this book about finding happiness in the modern age. Here in the 21st century, we're all encouraged to engage ourselves in current affairs and politics, which is very important but does very little to make us happy. With war, poverty, inequality, or any of the other things that upset us, it can be difficult to crack a smile some days. This book is an escape from the 21st-century blues and a way of finding reasons to let out a little giggle if possible.

Inside these pages (virtual or otherwise) are a lot of true stories that have been specially selected to bring joy and intrigue to you, the reader. There's a selection of stories about life-saving acts, little moments of silliness, finding purpose, charitable people - all sorts. Ideally, if you ever feel a little melancholy in the morning, you can pick up this book and skim through it to lighten the emotional load that day. This book is separated into three parts, based on the Tom Bodett quote at the beginning of this introduction.

Part One is about loving someone. This can be romantic love, family love, or love for a stranger - it doesn't matter. It's all about love and as the Beatles once put it, "All we need is love (doo-de-doo-de-doo)."

Part Two is concerned with having a purpose, finding something "to do" as Bodett puts it. Here you'll read stories of finding reasons to live and live well. Having a purpose ignites us and keeps us animated, no matter what that purpose is.

Part Three is about hope, which may just be the most important part of them all. We're told such awful news about the future that it's easy to give up hope. Political turmoil, climate change, economic disaster - it's all scary stuff, and we need a good reminder sometimes that there is hope. This part will be about looking forward to the future and contains stories about having a bit of hope and delight for what the future holds.

So, before this book becomes a part of your life for a short time, have a practice smile ready. The stories are written to be fun and may even include some jokes. With a bit of luck, these tales will give you a giggle, supply a smile, and provide some pleasantries.

Please enjoy.

PART ONE:
"...SOMEONE TO LOVE..."

Our first stop is all about love. We humans thrive on love, and things go wrong when we're deprived of it. As a society, we seek the love of other people and are drawn into relationships and family structures to help us feel fulfilled. We might even compound that with a furry pet such as a cat (if you like an animal that doesn't care about you) or a dog (if you like an animal that *only* cares about you).

In this chapter, we'll explore a selection of true stories on the concept of loving something or someone, that will hopefully inspire you and bring a smile to your face.

Never Say Never

"I'm giddy as can be." – Bob Harvey

In 1955, a young man by the name of Bob Harvey met a wonderful young lady called Annette Adkins while studying at high school. Bob was instantly smitten, his breath stolen from him at the mere sight of Annette as she strolled into the study hall. He recalls, "I looked and I said, 'Oh my gosh, here is the most beautiful woman I have ever seen in my life."

Their young romance blossomed, and Harvey took Adkins to the prom that same year in Woodbridge, Virginia. As many who are over the age of 18 know, young relationships are often torn apart by one of any number of factors, and this happened with Bob and Annette. Ambitions, colleges, and new friendships brought the relationship to its end - or so it seemed.

Bob and Annette both went on to get married to different partners, leaving the other behind as a high school memory. For the next 63 years, they both lived happy separate lives.

In 2017, Bob's wife sadly passed away, ending his long and very happy marriage. After a period of grieving, Bob decided that he'd 'Google' Annette, just to see how she'd been getting on. By a strange coincidence, he learned that her husband had also recently passed away. Bob decided to send her a card with his telephone number, and they got chatting again, rekindling their connection after more than 60 years apart.

Talking will only get you so far and Bob felt there was no time like the present for a good old-fashioned grand romantic gesture. He raced 500 miles toward Annette, stopping only for gas and a bouquet of carnations.

Bob arrived at her front door, presented the flowers, and gave her a smooch that was 63 years in the making. Picking up where they'd left off - a little grayer, with a few more wrinkles, and a lot more money - they quickly decided to marry. In 2019, at the age of 80, they married in a 1950s' style diner.

In an easy-going affair, they dressed casually and danced to Johnny Mathis, just like they did at prom all those years ago.

A Real PriMATE

This story is of a less conventional love. Not focused on romance nor familial affection, it's about the love for the natural world that many of us feel instinctually. We hate to see animals in pain, but how much does that love of nature compel us to do? Perhaps donate $10 to charity from time to time? Well, for Dian Fossey, it meant that she would give everything to save animals who could not save themselves.

Dian Fossey's story isn't a small-time story; in fact, her life was adapted into a movie called *Gorillas in the Mist*, starring 1980s icon Sigourney Weaver. But this doesn't stop it being a remarkable display of love.

Dian was born in 1932, in San Francisco, California. From an early age, she had a natural affection for animals, particularly primates. She became an occupational therapist after attending the University of California, and in 1966 decided to throw that out the window to travel to Africa.

She embarked on this remarkable journey to study mountain gorillas, a critically endangered species. Initially, she went to the modern-day Democratic Republic of Congo before moving her research to the Virunga Mountains of Rwanda, establishing the Karisoke Research Center in 1967.

Fossey cared deeply for the plight of the mountain gorilla, protecting the land of the research center with force and well-paid staff. Poaching was a huge problem in the park; even though it was illegal, park conservators were bribed to look the other way or were unable to stop anyone. Baby gorillas were being torn from their families, often with tragic and graphic consequences. To combat this, Fossey financed patrols to search the park, looking for signs of poachers. Their impact was impressive, helping to eradicate hundreds and thousands of traps, and bringing some poachers a well-deserved prison sentence.

Though her campaign against illegal poaching was important, Fossey was interested primarily in studying the remarkable primates. She conducted one of the most extensive and comprehensive long-term studies of mountain gorillas ever. She helped habituate gorillas to human presence and documented their behavior and social structures with remarkable precision.

Fossey formed a great bond with mountain gorillas, helping them see the work of her researchers as nonthreatening. Her fascination with every aspect of their lives and her deep love for the majesty of the species made Fossey the world-leading expert in mountain gorillas by 1980 when she was awarded a Ph.D. by Cambridge University.

The work was difficult, and many researchers left the project after not being able to withstand the difficult conditions and tough terrain. Even getting to the gorillas took dedication, never mind studying them. Fossey continued to dedicate her life to gorillas and in the end, she gave her life for them too.

In 1985, Fossey was murdered at the center, likely due to the strong actions she took against poachers. In the late 70s and early 80s, she had become extreme in her methods to stop poachers and would try anything from superstition to violence if it meant that they could be stopped. Someone decided to take her out of the picture, in all likelihood, to put a stop to her anti-poaching crusade.

Fossey's love for the gorilla led her to drop everything in aid of helping them. Her conviction is oddly inspiring and became all-encompassing for her. If you're interested, there's a lot more to discover about Fossey's life and legacy, some bizarre, some tragic, and much of it fascinating. Start with the movie, then go from there.

Poets Fall in Love Better Than Anyone Else

"I love you not only for what you are, but for what I am when I am with you." – Elizabeth Barrett Browning

There's a chance that you may not be aware of a period known as the Romantic period of poetry and literature. If you aren't, this isn't a command to go and read all of it. Really, some of it's quite sickly.

The Romantic poets wrote lovely, flowery poems about the essence of feeling, emotions, love, romance, and all the powerful senses we embrace in our lives. Running from the late 1700s to the mid-1800s, the period is remarkable for turning the world of literature on its head. Previously, the written word had mostly been rather scientific and dry.

Enter - Elizabeth Barrett Browning, a romantic poet born in 1806.

Elizabeth was a successful poet and something of a recluse. She was the eldest of 12 children and had written poetry since the age of 11. Her mother kept almost all of Elizabeth's poems and accidentally cataloged one of the world's most impressive collections of artistic works by a juvenile artist ever.

Her mother's support was crucial to Elizabeth's eventual success. Early 19th-century England was a tough time to be a woman. Women very rarely owned their own properties, were paid a tiny portion of men's salaries, and had no say in the politics of their world. The world of poetry was no exception to this inequality, and Elizabeth might have been discouraged had it not been for her mother's affection towards her work.

Elizabeth became sickly when she was 15 years old, with a series of afflictions that she would carry for the rest of her life. She continued to write poetry, mainly for the benefit of her family. Her father published a classic-style epic poem called *The Battle of Marathon*, written by Elizabeth at just 14 years old, along with a collection of her other poetry. The book was distributed to family members and her father continued to encourage Elizabeth to become a writer, so impressive was her early work.

She became a prolific and well-known poet in her late thirties, though was becoming more ill every year, developing tuberculosis. By societal standards, she was a spinster, an older woman who was destined to never marry. That is, until fellow poet Robert Browning wrote to her in 1844, to express his admiration for her work.

What followed was almost a year of courtship by letter, a first meeting in 1845, and a secretive marriage in 1846 away from all but one witness.

The couple went to live in Italy and their love deepened with time. Despite Elizabeth's age and health problems, she eventually gave birth to a son in 1849, age 43, a dangerous age to attempt birth in the 19th century. Elizabeth and Robert were famous and adored by the public. Elizabeth constructed elaborate and beautiful sonnets, inspired by her connection with Robert, which sold extremely well around Europe. She met the great literary artists of the age and inspired new generations of female writers.

Elizabeth's life story is incredible on two fronts. Firstly, Elizabeth exceeded the expectations laid out for women in the 19th century, cementing her legacy as one of the greatest ever romantic poets. Secondly, Elizabeth's success came with the support of her family and her husband. It was unusual that a wife would be highly encouraged by her spouse to be successful and work on her legacy. Robert gladly advised and encouraged, allowing Elizabeth to flourish at an age when most in society had discarded her. And that's how love should be!

Saving America One Person at a Time

During the 20th century, America battled within itself as it sought to overturn archaic race laws that unsettled the very fabric of society. Racism was allowed by law until the 1960s, and groups emerged that sought to embed white supremacy in the land of the free.

One example of this is the hate group the Ku Klux Klan, which gained notoriety for its violence and terrorist acts against Black people. For a time, the KKK seemed to have *carte blanche* to do whatever they wanted with minimum repercussions. People had been murdered, Black neighborhoods terrorized, and lovers kept apart by the terrorist organization. You'd have to be a particularly brave individual to engage with them without any fear of violent repercussions.

But this is precisely what African-American musician Daryl Davis has done since the 1980s. It started in 1983 when Daryl Davis was playing piano in a "White" bar in Maryland. A man approached Davis and told him that he'd "never heard a black man play as well as Jerry Lee Lewis," to which Davis informed him that Jerry Lee Lewis was taught by Black piano players and was a personal friend of his. The men got chatting before the patron disclosed that he was a member of the KKK. Davis didn't run away, or ridicule him; instead, they had a drink, exchanged contact information, and started a friendship.

The interaction inspired Davis. The man had left behind some serious prejudices by forming a friendship with Davis, all by just having a chat. Could Davis do it again? He procured contact information of Klan leaders from his new friend and set to work.

Davis then went on to engage directly with Klan members ever since and has helped many find their way out of the organization. He famously met with the Imperial Wizard of the Maryland branch of the KKK, concealing his race before the meeting. Supposedly the meeting started tensely but ended with Davis being gifted with the leader's robe as well as being asked to be godfather of the leader's daughter.

Davis remains friends with 20 former Klan members and claims to have directly, or indirectly, caused more than 200 people to leave the hate group. He's been gifted with over 25 robes from members and leaders, as well as a gold medallion holding the inscription "KKK-member in good standing." He has been present for many ex-members' weddings and funerals, while starting his own social media platform 'Minds', which aims to promote real and meaningful conversation between people with different points of view.

Davis shows us how love can do more than promote happiness - it can actually save us from hate. People don't hate for no particular reason. Davis believed that many of the KKK members were simply confused or had misunderstood something fundamental. By talking to them and introducing more love, Davis has had a real impact on a group that no longer has much influence.

Bob, the Savior

This tale of love truly saving a life is well documented in books and even a movie titled '*A Streetcat Named Bob*'. If you want to know more, there's plenty to watch or read.

James Bowen had a difficult start to his life. Like many children who move often and go through divorce, Bowen struggled to make friends at his changing schools. At a very young age, he became somewhat of an outcast and was bullied by children constantly. After his mother took him from Great Britain (aka United Kingdom) to Australia, he dropped out of secondary school with few prospects ahead of him.

In 1997, at the age of 17, Bowen decided to travel back to the UK, intent on making his fortune. Unfortunately, Bowen wasn't prepared for London. The city is tough and unforgiving, even more so if one has no qualifications. Bowen found himself homeless quickly, and to cope with the loneliness, began using heroin.

After a few years of drug abuse mixed with sleeping on the streets or in shelters, Bowen happened upon Bob. Bob had no home either and was seeking companionship. Bowen didn't know this at first, however…, because Bob was a cat.

Bowen saw Bob a few times over the course of a couple of days, assuming that the small ginger cat belonged to someone. After a short amount of time, however, it was clear that the feline was in some serious trouble. Bob was skinny and ill, and without intervention, he would die. Like most people, Bowen couldn't stand to see an animal in pain, so spent his last £20 to buy antibiotics for Bob, so that he'd live.

Bob decided to hang around after that. He put on some weight and accompanied Bowen at his busking spots, providing an extra pull for Bowen. The musician decided that now was the time to stop taking drugs; after all, Bob needed him to survive. He went onto a methadone program in the spring of 2007, which would seek to ween him off of heroin use. Within a couple of years, Bowen didn't even need that.

"I believe it came down to this little man. He came and asked me for help and he needed me more than I needed to abuse my own body. He is what I wake up for every day now." – James Bowen

Soon, Bob and James became a bit of a local celebrity couple. They'd regularly be spotted together on the No. 73 bus, and Bob would sit while James busked in the street. As videos emerged on YouTube of the pair selling copies of *The Big Issue*, a street newspaper that gives homeless people a way of generating income, their visibility increased.

Before long, they weren't just local celebrities, they were *celebrities*. Tourists came to see them, and newspapers began running their stories from 2010 on. From there, Bowen was brought to the attention of writer Garry Jenkins who saw the potential in the tale (or *tail*, get it?) and convinced Bowen that it was time to write a book.

Together, they created '*A Streetcat Named Bob*', which has gone on to sell more than ten million copies in the UK alone. The subsequent movie was released in 2016, with Bob playing himself in many of the scenes.

After Bob's death in 2020, tributes poured in from around the world to *The Big Issue*. Thousands grieved for the life-saving cat, who is remembered as something of a cult icon in the

UK. Just a small little ginger thing, that decided it should hang around just long enough to save someone's life.

Come One, Come All!

For Americans, spending Christmas and other holidays with their families isn't quite enough, so they celebrate Thanksgiving a month beforehand as well. This ensures that Christmas is full of awkward conversations as nothing new has happened since November! In all seriousness though, Thanksgiving remains a meaningful time for many Americans.

Family becomes especially important in this period and togetherness is emphasized. Putting aside differences, and focusing on celebrating bonds with those closest to us, makes the collection of holidays a time of great love for many Americans.

For two Americans, separated by 40 years and a few miles, Jamal Hinton and Wanda Dench, have a deeper relationship with the holiday than most. In 2016, Jamal, a then-17-year-old from Phoenix, Arizona, received a text message from an unknown number around November...

"Thanksgiving at my house, from Grandma"

Jamal has admitted that he was initially confused and there was a little bit of toing and froing, with some selfies thrown in to clarify who was messaging who. He learned that the sender was Wanda Dench, from Mesa, Arizona. With that cleared up, the ball was in Jamal's court. Many of us would have thought, "What a funny story," and left it at that, but Jamal isn't many of us. Wanda seemed nice enough, so he responded…

"Can I still get a plate tho?"

To which Wanda responded:

"Of course, you can. That's what grandma's do… feed everyone."

Jamal decided that he would take Wanda up on her offer and arrived at her house for Thanksgiving in November 2016. The Dench's always invite friends for Thanksgiving, so Jamal wasn't the only non-family member there, but he was surprised at how welcoming everyone was and found the whole thing equally brilliant and hilarious. Jamal documented the event on Instagram, gaining some attention from local news and users of the site, who laughed at the strange situation.

And that was that…

Until Jamal went back in 2017, this time with his girlfriend in tow. He then returned in 2018 and posted a picture on Instagram with the caption, "it's a tradition now." Long story short, the duo has met every year for Thanksgiving and has sparked an unlikely friendship over a strange, accidental text. In that time, Jamal has been there for Wanda after she lost her husband to COVID-19 in 2020 and Wanda remarked on *Today* how grateful she is to have met Jamal six years previously. Perhaps there doesn't have to be such a big divide between the generations; it just takes a bit of reaching out and having the nerve to say "yes.'"

> *"Jamal literally changed my life and my point of view on young generations about being open to friendships when you think you have nothing in common with somebody. But when you just sit and talk to them? Oh my gosh ... He's in my heart for life."*

Team Hoyt

If you ran in the famous Boston Marathon in the 2000s, then you would have been running alongside a formidable team that had more than 1,000 races under their belts.

That team would be Team Hoyt, Dick and Rick Hoyt, a father and son duo famous for their impressive race record.

Rick, the son, was born in 1962 with the condition cerebral palsy. Cerebral palsy is a grouping of movement disorders that occurs in childhood; for Rick, this manifested at birth after the umbilical cord became twisted around his neck, depriving his brain of oxygen. As a result, Rick faced a life without proper control of his limbs.

Rick's parents, Dick and Judy were informed that it would be sensible to institutionalize Rick and that he would be nothing more than "a vegetable." Unhappy with their doctor's rather grim outlook on their son's life, the loving parents decided that Rick deserved to come home with them. Rick was able to follow them around the room with his eyes, and they took solace in this. After seeking counsel from a more empathetic doctor at Boston Children's Hospital, they were advised to treat him like they would any other child.

Throughout Rick's childhood, he was educated by his mother, learning the alphabet quickly. At the age of 11, he was fitted with a state-of-the-art computer that would help him to communicate (another point for pushy parents who won't give up). Shortly after this, Rick attended public school for the first time.

Rick would go on to attend Boston University, securing a degree in special education and working on computer systems to aid communication for people with disabilities. By then (the 1990s), Rick was also an accomplished marathoner with several triathlons under his belt!

When Rick was 15 years old, a player on his high school's lacrosse team became paralyzed in a horrific accident. Rick wanted to prove that life doesn't end because of disability. He wanted to run a race together with his father to prove that fact.

Dick wasn't a runner; he was a retired Lieutenant Colonel at 36 years of age and had never been interested in doing any running. It has to be said that retiring at 36 does leave somewhat of a gap in your diary though, so Dick set about training with an insatiable drive to make his son happy after Rick told him:

"Dad, when I'm running, it feels like I'm not handicapped."

Dick began training by pushing bags of cement in a wheelchair while Rick was at school and became pretty accomplished, completing a 3.1 mile run in 17 minutes.

Between 1977 and 2016, Team Hoyt went on to finish more than 1,100 endurance events - and these weren't small fry either. That figure included 72 marathons and six triathlons. They even managed to run and bike across America in 1992, completing a frankly ridiculous 3,735 miles in just 45 days!

In 2016, the team parted ways, with Dick's age catching up with him. Rick continued, being pushed by a dentist by the name of Bryan Lyons until 2020 when Bryan unexpectedly passed away.

Unfortunately, both original members of Team Hoyt passed away in the 2020s, Dick at the age of 80 and Rick at 61. Considering that Rick was written off by a doctor as having no prospects to speak of, he lived quite a long life. How many parents, without much hope or medical knowledge, would have agreed and abandoned their son in an institution? How many would have had the intelligence and dedication to push back?

Rick's work has helped change the lives of people with severe disabilities, so that they may be able to communicate better with others. He's also shown, through his family hobby, that a disability doesn't mean the end of anything. All of this was only possible with a heck of a lot of love from his parents, who did everything they could to make sure he achieved the impossible.

There's Still So Much Left to Do

If all of humanity can agree on something, it's that cancer is a ***** (insert whatever expletive or insult you want to, everyone will agree). Unfortunately, as we journey through our lives, almost all of us will experience the effects of the brutal illness in some way. Either dealing with it ourselves or being there while someone we know must do so.

But if we know one thing about humans, it's that we're quite resilient. Some would even say stubborn. Now, armed with modern medicine improving at a staggering rate, we're better equipped than ever before to face the sickness head-on. One stands an improved chance if someone is standing there with you.

In July 2017, Jillian Hanson was diagnosed with stage two breast cancer at the age of just 25. Contending with the diagnosis meant a litany of emotions for Jillian. Though stage two means that the illness is still contained within one area, it is still growing and is very frightening. Her dreams of the future were now threatened, and she felt equal concern for Max Allegretti, her partner.

Jillian was aware that things were about to get difficult for the couple. Treatment is a grueling process, and she didn't know how long this might take, with no guarantee of success at the other end of it. She offered Max an out, a chance to leave and not suffer through it like she had to.

"I brought it to the table and told him that this was going to be a lot."

Not everyone can be the main support system for someone about to go through the most intense, difficult part of their life - but Max didn't question it for a second. Max instead decided to drop everything in his life, prioritizing Jillian above all else, to be her rock.

Jillian began chemotherapy in October 2017 and didn't finish until February of 2018. Chemotherapy is a wearying and demanding form of treatment that can sometimes be deadly by itself. Patients of chemotherapy will talk of exhaustion, intense vomiting, lack of appetite, and a variety of ghastly symptoms. Life is exceptionally difficult for those going through chemotherapy and that difficulty spreads like a ripple, affecting the loved ones around them.

While Jillian was, to put it politely, put through the wringer, Max stayed positive and kept up his promise to stay by her side. He'd take her to shows, get them tickets to the movies, cook for her, and be a spectacularly attentive partner.

"He took care of me every day and reminded me how beautiful I was - even as my hair thinned and fell out, and my skin turned white as a ghost."

February 28, 2018, rolled around, marking the end of Jillian's chemotherapy. This is often a time of uncertainty for patients. If you're lucky, chemotherapy will have done its job perfectly, but sometimes it's just the beginning of more torture and more chemo. Max wanted to ensure that whatever lay ahead, February 28, 2018, would be a happy day.

So, he proposed.

And she said yes (luckily).

Max knew he wanted to marry Jillian and that she wanted to be married too. The proposal was met with joy and tears, but a question mark lay over the whole thing. Jillian was still ill and faced a long period of tests, more treatment, and a smorgasbord of cancer-related appointments. She wouldn't have the energy and time to plan a wedding; it's stressful enough for healthy people.

Luckily, Max had met a wedding planner called Lauren Grech at a fundraising event for those diagnosed with breast cancer. Lauren's heart was melted by the story, and she decided that she would donate her time to Max and Jillian. She agreed to plan the whole thing for free, taking the organizational stress away from Jillian and Max who should just focus on recovery - and it didn't stop there.

Lauren utilized her impressive contacts in the industry to secure a few things for free such as:

- A wedding cake
- Jillian's dream dress
- The Sterling Ballroom to host the ceremony
- A wedding band
- A photographer
- A film maker
- A hair and makeup artist

The pair married in 2019, in a beautiful ceremony, and are still joined today. Jillian has received the all-clear from breast cancer and has emerged from the other end of the horrific ordeal. Thanks to the devotion shown by Max and the generosity of Lauren and her team of wedding wonders, Jillian was provided with the extra power to battle on through her cancer towards a fantastic life on the other side.

Educating the 20th Century

This story is, in part, about a very famous woman called Helen Keller. Keller was born in 1880, in Alabama, USA. At 19 months old, Keller suffered a bout of illness that robbed her of the ability to see and hear. She would later remark, in her autobiography, that it left her "at sea in a dense fog."

Until the age of seven, Keller communicated with her family in something called "home signs." This is the term for a made-up form of sign language that a child invents to communicate. It works in the context of their family, but it isn't recognized internationally. Unfortunately, this form of sign language brings a life that can't exist outside of the family home. Keller's parents recognized this and contacted the Perkins School for the Blind for help. The school sent Anne Sullivan.

Anne was a specialized and extremely successful educator; the school thought she would be the only person suitable to teach Helen. When Anne arrived at the family home, she ruffled feathers over politics, arguing with Keller's parents about their role in the Civil War and opinions on slavery. However, Helen seemed to like her, so she was kept around.

Helen quickly got to grips with Anne's style of teaching and progression was fast. Using a system of spelling words on Keller's palm, she was able to learn 575 words as well as understand multiplication and the braille system (a method of touch-reading for the blind). Anne realized that Helen was extremely intelligent and should be sent to the Perkins School to be educated properly. Anne said she'd accompany her and stay with her.

Keller's ability to adapt and learn despite being without two of her five senses was remarkable. Helen and Anne became famous, and their reputations intertwined with the Perkins School, which benefited. Anne took Helen to Radcliffe College (now Harvard University), where she earned a Bachelor of Arts degree, becoming the first deaf-blind person to do so.

Anne lived with Keller for the rest of her life. The two had a connection that was built on respect and education. Anne Sullivan was

Helen's link to the world that she couldn't see, teaching her how to be a part of it. Helen's ability to take that all on and run with it was remarkable, but beyond that the two loved each other deeply and were fantastic friends.

Helen went on to lecture at major universities (with the help of assistants like Anne), write 14 books on a variety of topics, advocate for women's rights, campaign for the rights of disabled people, and write speeches about the need for world peace. In all this, Helen wasn't just a person who'd lived with a debilitating condition. She was a person who *dominated* despite their debilitating condition. After her death, Helen Keller was voted by *TIME* magazine as one of the most important people of the 20th century.

Anne Sullivan is also well remembered for her connection with Helen Keller, and for helping someone so remarkable to tell their story and to live a full life. Their beautiful relationship has been portrayed in movies, television shows, plays, and musicals. Long may that continue!

Teaching Children
What the World Can't

When we are children, we're told by our parents and teachers to be *kind* to other people. This is a good thing, of course - as a society, we'd like our children to enjoy childhood without the worry of bullying or unkind behavior. Even better, they may then become kind adults who are nice to each other, which may help eradicate the unpleasantries of our world.

But typically, somewhere along the line, children lose a bit of their innocence. They see that the world isn't always kind, and it can leave them feeling confused or hurt. Through their wonderful, positive view of the world, such things as wars and violence can be disorientating.

In the 1960s, Pastor Fred Rogers saw this happening to children and wanted to help.

Fred Rogers, or Mr. Rogers, was a children's entertainer who ran an educational children's show called *'Mister Rogers' Neighborhood'* from 1968 to 2003, filming 895 episodes. He began as a Presbyterian minister, who eventually saw his calling as educating and mentoring children.

Through the 1950s and 1960s, Fred worked on several children's shows. He developed puppets as well as music and grew to understand the process behind creating an impactful show for kids. When he gained quite an amount of reputation at NET (National Educational Television, now PBS), he was asked if he had a show that he wanted to create and star in.

"I went into television because I hated it so, and I thought there was some way of using this fabulous instrument to be of nurture to those who would watch and listen."

The show was a kind show and very calm. Rogers had the same introduction every episode, by taking off his smart adult jacket and shoes, to be replaced by a cardigan and sneakers. He'd talk gently to the audience, the children, and tell them what the message of that week's episode was. It was always a positive message. Whether it was about loving who you are, or how to be tolerant, it was always important learning for children.

Fred Rogers was always proud of the show. It had a remarkably wide reach and ran into the 21st century. At its peak in the 1980s, it was attracting almost two million viewers, which is impressive for a show aimed at children. But Rogers' pride in the show went beyond the figures.

Rogers had a tough childhood and was bullied at school. Part of his motivation for creating 'Mister Rogers' Neighborhood' was to talk to those children who may be going through similar hardships. Rogers wanted to counsel those children from afar, helping them understand that such actions are wrong and that there's help available.

> "This is what I give. I give an expression of care. Every day to each child." - Rogers, speaking in Washington, to Congress.

The show ran on publicly funded money and as such, had a low budget. But the magic of the production was in Rogers' jaunty music, fun puppets, and overall welcoming feeling. The show is still regarded highly today, years after Rogers died in 2003, and serves as something of a template for companies that want to create a similar show.

Arguably, it would be impossible to create another 'Mister Rogers' Neighborhood'. The show worked because of Fred Rogers' character and genuine care for the children who were his audience. His life's work was defined by the show, and it left a lasting impression on many of America's population, so much so that he's often called "America's Grandpa."

The British Schindler

In 1909, a man by the name of Nicholas Winton was born in Hampstead, London. His family were German Jews, who were highly educated and had converted to Christianity, aiming to integrate into English life.

Winton received a good education as a teenager but failed to achieve any qualifications. He spent a few years in the early 1930s moving around Europe, working for banks so that he could gain some banking qualifications. Upon his return to London, he began work as a stockbroker. While making a decent living on the stock exchange, he became active in socialist activist groups and was particularly concerned about the developing situation in Germany.

During the 1930s, the English government adopted a policy known as appeasement. The policy was aimed at Adolf Hitler, the tyrannical, antisemitic fascist in charge of Germany. From 1933–39, Hitler had been taking dangerous steps into other countries' territories, threatening the safety of Europeans and world peace. Winton didn't like this and was greatly concerned about Hitler's actions. Like many at the time, he saw the potential in the crazed leader's words and felt that his actions spelled danger.

Abandoning a skiing holiday in 1938, Winton decided to go to Czechoslovakia, which had been invaded by the Germans. The British Jewish groups had begun a program called Kindertransport that aimed to extract Jewish children from Austria and Germany. Winton wanted to do the same thing in Czechoslovakia, which he knew housed many children who were in as much danger as those in Germany.

Winton used the name of the British Committee for Refugees from Czechoslovakia to take applications from parents who wanted their children taken to safety, in March 1939. He set himself up at his hotel and thousands of parents lined up outside his office, desperately seeking a safe place for their children to go.

Winton returned to London to raise funds for the children and to get the operation working. The transports were organized and donations trickled in to meet the 50 pounds per child requirement that the government had set. He worked around the clock; stockbroker by day and child rescuer by night. Winton located homes, hostels, and anywhere else that could safely care for the refugees from Czechoslovakia.

In March 1939, rescue operations began, and children were taken by plane, train, and ship away from the Czech lands that were being taken over by the Nazis. The last train left on August 2, 1939, as it became increasingly clear that World War II was about to erupt. There was a later train carrying 250 children that was refused permission to exit the country. All but two of those children were captured by the Nazis and killed.

Winton managed to find homes for at least 669 Jewish children, though historians agree that the actual figure is uncertain. Many children likely stowed away on the train or weren't accounted for, or who made their escape.

For 50 years after the miraculous escape of hundreds of children, Winton's actions were largely forgotten. It wasn't one of the main stories of the war, so to speak. In 1988, however, Winton was brought onto an episode of *'That's*

Life!', a TV consumer affairs program that broadcast in Britain. The show was immensely popular and received millions of viewers, and something special had been planned for Nicholas Winton.

Nicholas was sitting in the audience, as the presenter ran through a scrapbook of Winton's achievements. She introduced Vera Gissing, a British writer, who was one of "Winton's Children." Vera was positioned next to Nicholas Winton, and they shared a brief, tearful embrace as Vera thanked him for saving her life.

Another woman to his right then showed the pass that she had to wear upon arrival in London and similarly, thanked Winton for his efforts. With the audience applauding and Winton looking a little overwhelmed, the presented asked:

> *"May I ask, is there anyone in our audience tonight who owes their life to Nicholas Winton? If so, could you stand up please?"*

Approximately three dozen people rose to their feet around Nicholas in a beautifully poignant scene, as he turned to face them with a terrific mix of joy and sadness.

The episode has now been viewed countless times online and is well worth YouTubing if you have the time. Winton went on to be knighted by Queen Elizabeth II and he lived until 2015, when he passed away at the age of 106.

Nicholas isn't remembered for what he did with most of his life, but for what he did for a very small part of it. His work was miraculous and saved hundreds of people from the grips of the truest evil that Europe had ever seen. Not just anyone would have done this - it took Nicholas, who felt compelled, full of love and desire to help those who couldn't help themselves.

Saving Lives, While Lying Down

The truth of life is that, at some point, we will all need some medical intervention that is going to require some extra blood. Blood comes from donations and some types of blood are more valuable than others. If you've never donated blood before, it's worth checking your eligibility and seeing if you might be able to save some lives.

Blood donations are on the rise around the world, but the figures are still lower than we'd like. Only 7% of Americans are actively donating blood, while only 3.5–4% of Australians are doing so regularly. Europeans donate at a rate of 37%, which is an improvement, but the fact is that there is a need for more.

The reasons for donating blood are usually selfless. If you give blood, you're choosing to do something that very well may save someone's life soon…and that's it. It's not for financial reasons or kudos, it's out of love for other people. Or at least, that's what James Harrison felt during his years as "The Man with the Golden Arm."

James was born in 1951 in Australia. Unfortunately, his youth was marred with the necessity for serious surgery - life-threatening in fact. While in surgery, he received a large amount of blood that kept him alive. When he woke up from surgery, James was informed of how it went and what had saved his life. He recognized the importance of blood donations that day and vowed to donate when he was 18.

And, he did. James had a few donations in the first year he was allowed to, and his blood was analyzed to check blood type, suitability, etc. What was discovered was that James possessed a unique antibody that prevents newborn children from developing serious blood conditions. James was surprised but happy; he was in a position to do some good, just as a stranger had done all those years ago for him.

The doctors informed James that there were some further things to discuss. Blood donation can't happen too often as it poses risks to the donor, but plasma donation can happen regularly as it's replaced far quicker. James' incredibly rare antibodies were found in his plasma, so if he wished to, he could donate every few weeks.

So, from 1969 to 2018, James Harrison donated plasma every three weeks to provide crucial antibodies that help save babies' lives. James managed 1,173 donations over his "career," a record figure.

> *"I could say it's the only record that I hope is broken because if they do, they have donated a thousand donations."* – James Harrison

James was prohibited from donating further in 2018, due to age restrictions in Australia. Through the donations that rare people like James have given, millions of doses have been given to babies, preventing thousands of deaths and stillbirths.

It's a great story, in part because James has done so much by not doing very much. When reading his story, the question that pops into one's head is "Why don't I do that?" Well, why not indeed? The only reason that anyone gives blood or plasma is out of love and selflessness. We do so in the hope that it goes on to save lives, and James' donations certainly did.

Partners in Life and Work

Marie Curie is now a relatively well-celebrated name in the field of science, though she wasn't always well-known. Marie is known for being the first woman to ever win a Nobel Prize - and the first person to win two. Marie's work is celebrated but what is often forgotten is the passionate romance that enabled her discoveries.

Marie Salomea Sklodowska was born in Warsaw, Poland in 1867. Her father encouraged her in education, providing her with literature and education in physics and mathematics. She even attended an illegal night school with her sister, to progress their education further. It's important to remember that the mid-19th century was not an easy time for a woman to secure a good education. Societal pressures had a great effect on what a woman *should* be like.

In 1891, Marie moved to Paris with her sister to study at the Sorbonne, which housed the University of Paris. The university had given her a license to read physics and mathematical sciences. Curie was undeniably intelligent and had a bright future ahead of her, something which Pierre Curie saw from the first day he met her.

Pierre had been born in 1859 and possessed an equally incredible intellect. He held a master's degree by the age of 18 and earned his doctorate shortly after meeting Marie. Pierre took her in as a student in 1894 while working at the Sorbonne and they began dating shortly after. The idea of marriage flitted about in the air and after a year's courtship and endless love letters, the pair were married in July 1895. Interestingly, Marie eschewed the traditional white dress in favor of something darker, so she could wear it in the lab.

Post-marriage life would be transformative and propelled the duo into scientific stardom. While holding down a full-time job each and raising a child (later two children), they ran experiments on the new hot topic "radiation." Situated in a simple shed with sub-par equipment, they set about a series of complicated experiments that led to the discovery of "radium," winning them each a Nobel Prize in 1903. This made them the first couple to win the award.

To Pierre's disgust, however, the Prize didn't have Marie's name on it. He had to write a letter demanding her inclusion so that she could receive the award herself. Gender standards were shifting across the world at the time. Women had begun asking for their rights and equality with men, something Pierre seemed to understand better than most. He even turned down a cross of the Legion of Honor, a French order of merit, because Marie wasn't offered it as well.

Pierre unfortunately passed away in 1906 in a freak accident outside a reunion event he'd attended, being hit by an out-of-control truck. Marie was struck by overwhelming grief, naturally. She'd lost her partner in love and work. They shared passions like few couples get to, an idea that Pierre echoed in one of his letters to Marie, hoping to persuade her to accept marriage:

"It would, nevertheless, be a beautiful thing in which I hardly dare believe, to pass through life together hypnotized in our dreams: your dream for

your country; our dream for humanity; our dream for science.

Marie was offered Pierre's professorship at the Sorbonne, which was the first time they'd given a woman the role of professor. She later commented, "…there have been some imbeciles to congratulate me on it," as if the roles had been reversed and Pierre was to be forgotten in the wake of her achievements.

Marie went on to win another Nobel Prize for the discovery of polonium and continued work on radiation and its possibilities. She also wrote Pierre's biography, detailing his life before he met Marie, their courtship, marriage, and professional relationship. Marie died in 1934 due to long-term damage from radiation.

Marie and Pierre Curie's work founded the field of atomic science, and all uses of radiation, good and bad, have come from their obsessive work. Their relationship was rarely fraught; they were extremely happy and head-over-heels in love, working toward a shared dream. With all that excellence, it leaves us to wonder whether perhaps they'd just *occasionally* bicker about what restaurant to eat at that weekend…

The Savior of Country Music

"Hello, I'm Johnny Cash."

This is the now-famous opening line to hundreds upon thousands of concerts performed by the legendary country musician Johnny Cash. Cash performed for approximately half of a century, providing an incredible back catalog of music that covered silly stories, tales of crime, regret, Native American rights, and heartfelt ballads of pain. Long story short, Johnny Cash is one of the most beloved musicians of all time, even 20 years after his death.

Johnny had a difficult childhood, as many who grew up in the 1930s in America did. The stresses of the crashing New Deal era economy mixed with a turbulent family life. His father was quite a controlling, abusive man who put pressure on all members of the family. Johnny and his siblings worked cotton fields, sawed wood, and did anything else that might bring some money into the family home. Johnny lost his brother and best friend in 1944, in a tragic accident at the sawmill.

Johnny's career as a musician took off in the mid-1950s after he'd completed service in the Air Force. His first marriage to Vivian Liberto bore a child, so he tried to make money through sales, which he was rubbish at. By 1955, however, he'd signed for Sun Records and had begun to make it as a rockabilly country star. Johnny played with Elvis Presley, Jerry Lee Lewis, and countless other stars of the era, and he became extremely famous. Songs like 'Walk the Line,' 'Ring of Fire,' and 'Folsom Prison Blues' spent weeks in the charts and are still staples to this day as their lyrics are timeless and poignant.

He didn't deal with fame well, however. Years of touring, philandering, drug taking, and drinking led to a messy divorce from Vivian in 1964. Tour friends and fellow musicians didn't acknowledge that Johnny was becoming addicted to drugs, taking amphetamines almost constantly to stay awake for his concerts.

Johnny's behavior worsened after the divorce, with his crippling drug addiction taking hold. In

1965, he set fire to 508 acres of forest while trying to keep warm on a camping trip and was arrested for smuggling prescription drugs from Mexico into America. At this time, he had hit an all-time low. Shows were canceled and, as often happens in circles that have heavy drug use, his friendship group was dwindling.

Who knows what would have happened had June Carter not become a major part of Johnny's life? The Carter family were a well-known country family who had an impressive back catalog of songs that were loved across America, including by Johnny, who was a fan. He met June while on tour in the 1950s when they were both in separate marriages. June saw Johnny's addiction developing earlier than most had and held a great deal of sympathy for him. She helped him when his career and life had collapsed. Johnny said of June:

"She has saved my life more than once."

In 1968, Johnny proposed to June, and they married in Franklin, Kentucky. Shortly after, Johnny kicked the drugs and outrageous behavior, something that he credits entirely to

June's influence and the stability she brought to his life.

As country stars it was only right that they perform several duets such as 'Jackson' and 'It Ain't Me, Babe.' They built a reputation as something of a superstar celebrity couple that went beyond music. Johnny became an activist for Native Americans in the 1960s and 70s as well as an advocate for prison reform, even going so far as to meet with President Nixon in 1972 to discuss the subject.

The couple worked and lived together for several decades, having a child and producing music. They aged together and, by the turn of the millennium, could look back on three happy decades of marriage and sobriety. Johnny's music had become more solemn and melancholic at the end of his life.

In May 2003, June Carter died at the age of 73. She'd told Johnny to keep working after her death, so he recorded another 60 songs over the next four months. He performed for the last time in July of the same year and gave a brief tribute to his late wife:

"The spirit of June Carter overshadows me tonight with the love she had for me and the love I have for her. She came down for a short visit from Heaven to visit with me tonight to give me courage and inspiration like she always has... I thank God for June Carter. I love her with all my heart."

Johnny died in September 2003, a mere four months after June. Those close to Johnny said that he couldn't function after June's death and kept working to keep himself busy. June's (and her family's) involvement in Johnny's life saved it, no doubt. Excessive drug use has killed many musicians before and it would certainly have taken him, the way he was going. By saving him, June allowed the two of them to enter the annuls of music history together, rather than be forgotten country musicians of yesteryear.

Still Talking About
Them 500 Years Later

In the Agra District of Uttar Pradesh, India stands one of the world's most recognizable and awe-inspiring structures. With vast ivory columns that frame a specific, intricately-crafted domed palace, the Taj Mahal is remarkable.

Recognized as one of the seven new wonders of the world by UNESCO, the Taj Mahal attracts between seven and eight million people every year. It stands as the greatest construction of the Indian Mughal Empire that spanned 1526–1867. Its construction began in 1632 and its full construction was finished in 1653. Its beauty is described by Indian poet Rabindranath Tagore as "a teardrop on the cheek of time," and the story behind its inception helps provide context to the incredible structure.

The Taj Mahal is not actually a palace, nor is it a temple. It is instead a mausoleum, a place of grief. The Mughal emperor Shah Jahan commissioned it to be both the resting place and memorial to his wife, Mumtaz Mahal.

The future emperor Jahan spotted Mahal in the markets of Agra, where she was selling wares such as jewels, beads, and silks in 1607. The two were teenagers at the time, Mahal being 14 and Jahan being 15. Reportedly, as teenagers are wont to do, Jahan fell deeply in love with Mumtaz Mahal, who had some political standing of her own as an aristocrat. For five years, she largely ignored his advances or suggestions of marriage, but as they entered their twenties, they married.

As was customary for the Mughal Empire, Mumtaz was actually the emperor's third wife. His other wives, Qandahari Mahal and Akbarabadi Mahal were arranged by his father. Reportedly Jahal wasn't interested in his arranged marriages, but he was infatuated with Mumtaz. The two were inseparable, following each other everywhere. Mumtaz even accompanied him onto the battlefield when she was pregnant and was regularly entrusted with the royal seal.

The two enjoyed a two-decade-long marriage until, in 1631, Mumtaz died due to complications during childbirth. Emperor Jahan was completely inconsolable, putting the royal court into a period of mourning for two years. He called for the greatest architects and artists of the Mughal Empire (of which there were many) to help design a grand tribute to his life companion. After completing designs, 20,000 artisans helped build the Taj Mahal, along with 1,000 or so elephants.

As a building, it's simply breathtaking. It combines artistic influences from the Early Modern Islamic world including Persian, Ottoman, and Mughal styles. It takes influence from the Quran's description of heaven, and it's supposed to represent balance and harmony. When one stands in the center, the sun can be spotted rising and setting on the north and south corners during the summer and winter solstices.

The building now represents more than two people who adored each other. It's now a memorial to a time when Islamic empires' reach was colossal, and their influence unparalleled. The empires boasted excellent scientific work, mathematical breakthroughs, and artistic endeavors that were displayed within the Taj Mahal.

PART TWO:
"...SOMETHING TO DO..."

Onto Part Two then. This section is all about finding purpose in our lives, as a way of being joyful and finding happiness. That doesn't mean securing yourself a gray, drab nine-to-five position, but rather busying yourself with something that brings you peace and joy.

In this section, we'll present some true stories of people finding purpose in their activities, hobbies, jobs, and interactions with others.

Moore Than Expected

Of course, none of us want to have to think back to 2020 and the horrible events of the global COVID-19 pandemic, but we're going to revisit that time for this famous story.

From March 2020 onward, life became disrupted by coronavirus, a viral disease that affects people's ability to breath properly and can be deadly. As the illness spread across the world, the World Health Organization advised that people isolate themselves from others to help prevent further infections. Depending on where you were living at the time, your interpretation of the affair will be different from others. Some countries suffered high death rates due to many factors, while others managed through with lower rates. The overriding truth was that it was unpleasant and 2020 in particular was a difficult year for many.

In the United Kingdom, life was a struggle. Being one of the later countries to commit to a lockdown, the virus was in full flow by the time action was taken and many people were suffering. Combined with an economy that had been limping through the last decade, British people were very unhappy during the lockdown. The mood was bleak as the infection rates soared and the country's NHS struggled to cope.

If you ask someone from the UK about notable events from the pandemic, then they'll likely mention scotch eggs, half-price meals at restaurants, and Captain Tom Moore. Moore was a retired British Army officer who approached his 100th birthday during the pandemic. On April 6, Tom (now facing a less celebratory birthday than he may have liked) decided that he'd start a small fundraiser for NHS Charities Together, that supported staff members in the NHS.

He aimed to complete 100 lengths of his garden, ten lengths a day. The garden was 82 feet in length, a suitably demanding goal for someone pushing into triple figures. Tom's '100th Birthday Walk' for the NHS was the name of the event. Tom began.

He wanted to raise £1,000 in donations for the NHS, which was achieved within four days.

British news outlets grabbed hold of the story quickly, desperate for some good news at such a time, and included links to the online fundraiser. The target was upped to £5,000 but had to be increased to £500,000 by 12 April, on which day the fundraiser secured £1,000,000.

By 16 April, Tom had finished his fundraiser. But, sensing how successful it could be, he announced he wouldn't be stopping there and would complete a second hundred lengths! By the time he reached his birthday, Tom had raised £32,796,475 for NHS charities, which was a record for the JustGiving website. Tom received 150,000 birthday cards on his 100th birthday and was honored in many ways, including eventually being knighted by the then-monarch, Queen Elizabeth II. He set up his own foundation shortly after the conclusion of his JustGiving page, called the Tom Moore Foundation, now run by his family.

His story helped give a little boost to many people who were suffering through the pandemic with loneliness and sickness. Ultimately, his story is well remembered from that period for good reason: he helped bring a small smile to many people's faces. The donations from across the world showed how much the event had done to unite people and display what a useful way it was to spend his 100th birthday.

Tom died in 2021 from pneumonia while testing positive for COVID-19 and was declared a British national hero.

Paving the Way
Forward with Books

If you were to survey 100 people on what they think about Dolly Parton, approximately 100 of them would respond with one of three words: "inspiring," "entertaining," or "role model."

If you have lived under a rock for most of your life or are disgustingly young, then you may not know much about Dolly Parton. Dolly is a country music singer who helped bring country songs into the world of pop, which she has successfully done for decades. She wrote hits like 'Jolene' and '9 to 5' which are well-known standards of the music world.

However, when people become famous, it can go to their heads. Arrogance sets in, or a sense of entitlement eats away at the humbler aspects of someone's personality. Comedian Pamela Stevenson describes it as a "re-entry problem," when talking about her husband Billy Connolly returning from touring and adoring fans. But for Dolly Parton, this doesn't seem to be the case, which likely comes from her background.

Dolly was one of 12 children born into a poor farming family in Tennessee in 1946. The country had emerged from a decade-long depression and World War II. It was a tough time for her family, but Dolly displayed a remarkable knack for singing and music from a very young age. The moment she left formal education in 1964, she traveled to Nashville to pursue her career as a singer.

Dolly quickly gained recognition as a star to watch, being something of a protegee of Porter Wagoner, a huge star at the time. She set out on her pathway in 1974 and became a huge success. She won awards in 1975 and '76 as Female Singer of the Year by the County Music Association and the hits piled up. Grammys were handed out to Dolly like candy, but they were richly deserved for her catchy, fun, poignant, and joyful music. Of course, she became a film star as well, as many of the big stars did in the 1980s, contributing soundtracks as well. Dolly's success only continued, and she still makes music to this day that sells in the hundreds of thousands.

Dolly's career certainly made her happy, and she has exuded positivity from day one, but she chose a rewarding path of philanthropy that few who achieve her level of wealth do. In 1988, she set up the 'Dollywood Foundation', named after her theme park in Tennessee. It started as a program to help children in the region achieve in education. By 1995, it had morphed into the 'Imagination Library', and its reach extended, providing free books to children all over the world from birth until they begin school.

The undertaking of the charity is huge and very well thought out. Dolly's vision was that poorer families, who often can't afford many books, are assisted in improving the literacy of their children at early ages. In the short term, it provides immediate resources for those families and opportunities for bonding and home education. In the long term, Dolly hoped that it would help boost literacy rates among young children. Studies have shown that participants in the Imagination Library have consistently higher literacy rates when they start school than their peers.

As of 2023, the Imagination Library has donated over 200 million books to children all over the world and shows no signs of stopping. The organization accepts donations, but it sprang up out of Dolly's desire to make a tangible, very real difference in young people's lives. When she was young, her father was unable to read, which wasn't uncommon in America for people in his generation, particularly farmers. In Dolly's eyes, everyone should be able to share in the joy of reading and writing. The program recognizes that the best time to share that joy is when we're very young and being read to by parents.

It's difficult to source exactly how much money Dolly has now contributed to the program, but she continues to provide financial aid to other causes as well. In 2020, she donated $1 million to COVID-19 research and the next year provided $700,000 to help victims of flooding in Tennessee. Across two donations, she donated more than most people will ever be able to earn in their lives - and she's donated far more than that!

Parton's philanthropy is, unfortunately, remarkable. Careers in entertainment can be difficult, and many people disappear into their own world when they're in that arena. Dolly managed to locate an opportunity to garner meaning from her success. Her impact is genuine, and the Imagination Library program shows no signs of slowing down.

Almost 100, and
He's Still Got It!

For British people, certain days are guaranteed to have a serious impact. The day that Queen Elizabeth II died was a huge event with a period of national mourning. John Lennon's murder seemed to bring the world together. If the country ever runs low on tea, there'll potentially be riots. Yes, Britain can be very emotional about certain things and certain people, yet even some of those figures can be divisive. People have opinions about the royal family and about famous figures like John Lennon, so it's difficult to predict someone's reaction. If you want a guarantee that you'll elicit a strong positive emotional response from a British person, though, just say the words "David Attenborough."

David Attenborough is the definition of the phrase "national treasure" and is Britain's universal grandfather. David boasts a career as a wildlife documentary maker that is almost 70 years long and still going even though he is now

97 years old. He also has a talented brother, Richard Attenborough, who starred in *Jurassic Park* and directed *Gandhi*, winning an Oscar. The Attenboroughs must be a shoo-in for the "most competitive dinner table at Christmas" award.

David Attenborough was born in 1926, in Isleworth, Middlesex. As a young child, he displayed an interest in the natural world, collecting fossils and other specimens of interest. In 1936, he attended a lecture by "Grey Owl," a conservationist, with his brother Richard, and they became taken with the idea of conservation. Richard said of that day:

> "[David was] bowled over by the man's determination to save the beaver, by his profound knowledge of the flora and fauna of the Canadian wilderness and by his warnings of ecological disaster should the delicate balance between them be destroyed. The idea that mankind was endangering nature by recklessly despoiling and plundering its riches was unheard of at the time, but it is one that has remained part of Dave's own credo to this day."

David spent his formative years being educated at a prestigious grammar school, studying natural sciences at Cambridge, completing his national service in the Navy, and marrying his wife, Jane. In 1952, he joined the BBC and helped produce TV quiz shows on nature, and a series about folk music. He didn't have to do this for long, however, as by 1955 David had presented two shows about the natural world, kickstarting his long career.

At the risk of sounding glib, Attenborough spent the next 70 years making some of the most influential documentaries of all time. He has traveled the world, viewing the best natural sights available, and coordinating teams that have successfully captured rare animals on film all over the world. Bizarre phenomena, never before recorded by a camera, have been caught by Attenborough's camera crews and brought to television screens for generations now.

His most notable series include 'The Living Planet, The Trials of Life, The Blue Planet, Planet Earth'… and honestly, the list goes on to end up with a list of more than 100 documentaries on the natural world. Attenborough has received countless awards and acknowledgments including a knighthood, several BAFTAs,

Emmys, and a research boat that is named after him. It's all very impressive and comes from a genuine love for the natural world. Attenborough has been living his dream of working in this field for longer than many get to live.

In recent years, however, his work has taken on a new purpose. Inspired by that first lecture by Grey Owl and by the ignorance of the 20th century, Attenborough produces a lot of his documentaries to display the impact of human activity on the natural world. The worsening climate crisis is now at the forefront of Attenborough's documentaries, and he often launches appeals directly to the camera, pleading with the audience to act in whatever way they can.

As a patron of the WWF, the Worldwide Fund for Nature, Attenborough has been a vocal advocate, desperate to help the preservation of the natural world. In recent years, such advocacy has had an impact as corporations, individuals, and governments have begun working together to reverse the damage done.

Attenborough's story is one of pure passion. Most people change jobs or careers a few times in their lives as desires and needs change, but David Attenborough has only been concerned about presenting the natural world as it is to his viewers. There's something inspirational about that, and there's lots of inspiration to be found in his incredible documentaries.

"I wish the world was twice as big – and half of it was still unexplored."

Keeping Yourself Occupied

The Renaissance period was a unique time from the late 15th century to the early 17th century during which Europe became preoccupied with discovery, art, and thinking. The word "Renaissance" literally means "rebirth" and is about the rebirth of classical artistic endeavor after several centuries without that sort of pursuit.

The period brought such fantastic art the *'Last Supper '*and the *'Mona Lisa'*. People sought to understand the truth about human anatomy for the first time, and early designs for modern equipment, aircraft, and solar power were even designed in the period. And it's worth pointing out that everything mentioned in this paragraph was conceived of by one man: Leonardo da Vinci.

Da Vinci was an Italian artist who was born in Florence in 1452. Culturally, he couldn't have been in any more important place; Florence was essentially the birth of the Renaissance. He was raised in a relatively poor family before receiving tutelage in painting by Andrea del Verrocchio, then moving to work as a painter for the Duke of Milan at the age of 30.

It was in Milan that da Vinci produced some of his most famous works including the 'Last Supper', 'The Vitruvian Man'', and The Virgin of the Rocks'. After 17 years in Milan, he moved on to work as a military architect and engineer, helping to develop the science of cartography (as you do), before moving back to Florence in 1503 and painting the Mona Lisa (again, as you do). When da Vinci left Florence in 1508, his artistic endeavors petered out and he focused his attention on science while working in France, where he died in 1519.

Now, Leonardi da Vinci's life as an artist is incredible enough. Most artists would be happy to produce one excellent piece of work that brings them recognition, reverence, fame, fortune, or something akin to that. Of the 15 or so paintings that we have left that were painted by da Vinci, all of them are considered masterpieces. The latest painting to be sold of da Vinci's was the Salvator Mundi, which sold for more than 450 million dollars, making it the most expensive painting of all time. Wherever his work is displayed in the modern world, people flock to see it. The man had an undeniable eye for beauty and became absorbed in the Renaissance artistic movement, managing to secure himself as the face of the movement.

He wasn't just an artist though. Perhaps as impressive, if not more, is his journaling. Leonardo da Vinci kept a series of journals, diaries, and scribblings that he'd completed. He very rarely wrote anything in them about his personal life; it doesn't seem like it particularly interested him. Instead, the diaries were more of a record of what he was thinking. And what was he thinking about? Da Vinci was thinking about concepts that wouldn't come to fruition for many centuries. He was quite ahead of his time!

The current estimate is that da Vinci created between 20–28,000 pages of notes and sketches across 50 notebooks. He would discuss painting sometimes, but generally, his interest was in other subjects. He might write and discuss philosophy and politics, before shifting to warfare and engineering.

Some of what was found in his notebooks is listed here:

- *'The Vitruvian Man'*, is a remarkably precise sketching of the human body, showing how well-balanced and perfectly proportioned it is. He wrote underneath "…man is the model of the world."
- A new design for a type of church. He became obsessed with the acoustics in churches, forever finding it annoying that preachers' voices could rarely be heard at the back of the church. So, he designed a lecture hall in the shape of an amphitheater (most lecture halls are now designed in similar ways).
- On the subject of architecture, Leonardo submitted a design for a bridge to Sultan Bayezid II of the Ottoman Empire. The bridge measured 900 feet across and was dismissed instantly as impossible. In 2001, the designs were used to build that bridge in Norway, which stands to this day.
- Most famously, da Vinci produced several designs for flying machines. He was obsessed with the idea and wrote more than 35,000 words and produced more

than 500 sketches on the subject. We're unsure if the designs would work, but his designs were remarkably impressive.

There's much more hidden in his secretive diaries and it is probable that even more has been lost to time. It's also worth mentioning that da Vinci wrote a lot of this in a backward script so you had to read it with a mirror to understand it!

Ultimately, da Vinci kept busy. He embodied the vision of the Renaissance man, the enlightened individual who could do it all. His work has genuinely changed the face of the world, especially the artistic one. He was obsessed with thinking, science, art, and the combination of all disciplines into one. Remember that he didn't even start his "career" as it were, until he was 30. So, if you're not there yet, you still have time to be recognized as a genius. If you're past that age, apologies for making you feel bad - blame Leonardo.

Making a Molehill
Out of a Mountain

The question you get asked at parties the most, is horrible, isn't it?

"What do you do?"

We reduce our identity to our job at that moment as we give the expected answer, "I'm a quantity surveyor" or "I'm currently unemployed." The thing is, we're more than our jobs. Our identities are made up of several things such as our opinions, our hobbies, our passions, and our commitments.

In the case of Dashrath Manjhi, he has come to be defined by something that he wasn't paid to do but was a job he gave himself. Manjhi was born in a poor village called Gehlaur in Bihar, India in 1934 and like most people in the village had very little material wealth. The village has few resources and is located on a plain, surrounded by large, insurmountable mountains. Bringing food and supplies in took a long time, even to this day.

Dashrath was unlucky enough to be born into the bottom of India's caste system, as part of a Musahar family. Those at the bottom of the system could expect unfair treatment, racism, and a generally difficult life. At a very young age, Dashrath ran away from his family home to the far larger city of Dhanbad, some 155 miles away. His idea was to work in the large coal mines and earn some wealth. Though he didn't return to the village as a wealthy man, he came back happier and married Falguni Devi. Dashrath settled into a life as an agricultural laborer, looking forward to starting a family.

Due to the village being surrounded by steep mountains made from quartzite, any access to a bigger nearby town was almost impossible. The mountain had long provided problems for the people, lengthening journeys to a point far beyond inconvenient, but was also dangerous. The cliff face is extremely steep. Many have fallen from the mountain over the centuries, leading to deaths and severe injuries. Unfortunately, in 1959, Falguni fell from the mountain and suffered fatal wounds, which a doctor was not able to tend to in time.

Many blamed the mountain for Falguni's death, including Manjhi, who vowed to do something about it. Manjhi informed the villagers that he was going to cut a roadway into the mountain that would render the village more accessible. The villagers mainly laughed at the proposal; it seemed impossible and would require an almighty amount of dedication. Manjhi said that he felt compelled to do something for society, and what better way to contribute to his village?

"When I started hammering the hill, people called me a lunatic, but that steeled my resolve."

Manjhi spent 22 years completing the job. In that time, he carved a 360-foot-long path, 25.26 feet deep and 29.86 feet wide, which formed a functional, working road that reduced the journey to the town drastically. It wasn't only for his village; some 60 villages gained easier access to healthcare and work that was only a few miles away.

"Though most villagers taunted me at first, there were quite a few who lent me support later by giving me food and helping me buy my tools."

Manjhi died in 2007 at the age of 70 from cancer and was awarded a state funeral by the

Government of Bihar. He's been referred to as "the mountain man" since and is something of a revered figure in the region. Indian film and television have paid homage to his story with several renditions, including one documentary. After Manjhi's death, the path that he carved was officially made into a road, with supporting infrastructure, and is commonly used to this day.

There's something in this story that inspires the soul. No one asked Dashrath to do this, he took on the task himself for no pay other than the knowledge that his village would be better off if he did it. No doubt finding motivation from his young wife's death, he had the drive to do something incredible and literally move mountains for his loved one.

Going Against Their
Worst Judgment

Unfortunately for some people, something goes drastically wrong in life, and they end up serving time in prison. Prisoners often have jobs, but many prisons don't offer payment for those positions. In prison, it's easy for people to fall into habits that are unhelpful or possibly dangerous, but like everywhere in life, there are opportunities to show your moral character.

It will always be assumed that prisoners and prison guards despise each other and are out to get each other. This isn't always the case. Television and movies perpetuate stereotypes about cruel and overpompous guards in contrast to conniving prisoners out to cause harm. These stereotypes don't always play out and there are instances of incredible dynamics within prisons, though these don't often receive attention from the media.

In 2020, three prisoners at Gwinnet County Jail called Terry Loveless, Walter Whitehead, and Mitchell Smalls were dubbed heroes by thousands of social media users and the sheriff for their courage and selfless behavior, saving a life in doing so.

On July 10, Deputy Warren Hobbs came to work as usual. Described by most inmates as a quiet man and respectful, he was relatively well-liked in Housing Unit 3M, which he oversaw. His shift started normally, with a count of the inmates at approximately 6 p.m. before he went to say hello to another deputy. After this, things started to change for Hobbs.

He initially felt a small headache, followed by a rapid increase in body temperature. Hobbs walked to the recreation yard outside and began fanning himself with his hat to cool himself down. His vision blurred as he stumbled back to his desk, and he began to sweat profusely. He was worried that something was very wrong. Inmate Smalls was watching him the whole time. Smalls' testimony is best heard in his own words:

> *"I was randomly awake. I'm in the only room where you can see behind the deputy's desk. I looked out my window and saw him slouched down and he kept slouching more and more. I pushed my*

intercom button and rang my bell, but Deputy Hobbs didn't reply. I knew something wasn't right, I was hoping the deputy wouldn't fall from his chair, because it's high, but he fell. His head slammed on the floor and there was so much blood."

Hobbs was in a bad way; the fall to the floor had incapacitated him and he was bleeding profusely. Smalls sprang into action and began pounding on the door and screaming at the deputy. He bellowed for the nearby inmates to wake up and do the same and before long, an orchestra of bellowing inmates were screaming for the deputy to wake up.

The noise stirred the deputy briefly, though he was barely able to recognize what was going on. In his haze, he assumed that he was sitting at his desk still, rather than on the floor. Slipping in and out of consciousness, he locked eyes with the inmates in Unit 617, Whitehead and Loveless. Assuming that something must be wrong, or perhaps something simply connected with him at that stage, he managed to get to the button that opened the doors to the unit before falling back down.

Whitehead and Loveless sprinted out of their doors toward the deputy. Whitehead later reported that "...his color had changed and there was blood everywhere." Fearing for his life, the prisoners picked up the deputy's ringing phone and said he was in serious trouble and needed help, while desperately using the radio to reach other deputies.

The inmates stayed with Hobbs, but he basically remembers none of their interventions. He came to as he was being stretchered away and had an EKG placed on his chest. After tests, it was discovered that he was suffering a heart attack that had been suppressed by an aspirin he had taken for his headache earlier. The prisoners, especially Smalls, were crucial to his survival. Had Smalls not raised the alarm, then a very different story would be being told about Deputy Hobbs.

The inmates had their pictures and the Gwinnet County Sheriff's Office posted on Facebook to make public their gratitude to the men who had rushed to the aid of the deputy:

> *"These inmates came to his aid because our deputy, like most law enforcement officers, treats people*

*with the dignity they deserve. These inmates had
no obligation whatsoever to render aid to a
bleeding, vulnerable deputy, but they didn't
hesitate. Many people have strong opinions about
law enforcement officers and criminals, but this
incident clearly illustrates the potential goodness
found in both."*

The prisoners have all publicly given statements
about their gratitude for the public's response
and discussed the effect of the incident on their
lives. All three of the men were in prison for
nonviolent drug offenses. The men spoke of
feeling proud of themselves and that they
would value their lives more. Their actions
spoke volumes about their ability to think on
their feet and function despite an escalating
emergency. What we do isn't only about our
jobs, but about our actions that help give us
meaning and joy for the future.

How to Break Records
for Kindness

Americans are voracious consumers of entertainment, particularly sports. The nation's favorites are American football and baseball, but there are a great many other sporting events that attract millions of viewers. One of these is WWE, or wrestling, which is the eighth-most popular spectator sport in the country.

Wrestling makes superstars out of the exceptionally strong, athletic, and bendy people who take part. Making it in wrestling can also provide opportunities for later life, as Dwayne Johnson has proven by moving from WWE legend to global movie superstar. One who looks to follow in Johnson's footsteps is John Cena, who seems to be close to throwing in the towel on an illustrious wrestling career (while appearing in major movies such as 2023's *Barbie*).

Cena has been at the top of his game for the whole of the 21st century, proving himself as the world champion on 16 separate occasions. His cool persona, aggressive performances, and a very impressive array of muscles have made him a favorite of young people around the world. Cena adores his fan base and is well known for giving them meaningful time with him, particularly if they haven't got much time left.

This brings us to the Make-a-Wish Foundation, a fantastic charity that facilitates incredible opportunities for children suffering from terminal illnesses. The wishes vary greatly from a trip to Disneyland, a huge shopping spree, or meeting their favorite celebrity. The foundation secures funding so that the family can be aided in providing a remarkable experience for the child that fulfils their wish. Celebrities often prove difficult to secure. They're people with busy schedules and lives, so organization can be tough. But not when it comes to John Cena.

John Cena currently holds the Guinness World Record for the most Make-a-Wish wishes granted, which he was awarded on July 19, 2022. Cena's meetings with the children are praised as he puts a lot of work into ensuring that they're meaningful, rather than tokenistic.

Cena brings his championship belts with him and spends time getting to know whoever has requested him.

> *"I can't say enough how cool it is to see the kids so happy, and their families so happy, I truly want to show them that it's their day... I just drop everything. I don't care what I'm doing."*

Cena is, by far, the most requested celebrity from Make-a-Wish and is the only person who has fulfilled more than 200 wishes. He's also used his platform as a global superstar to push messages of kindness and has publicly led anti-bullying campaigns across America. Cena has made sure that the focus is always on the time that he contributes. Time is non-refundable and is the most precious thing to donate. Behind the huge, behemoth of a man who throws people around inside of the ring is a very kind-hearted soul who still receives, and attends dozens of Make-a-Wishes requests every year.

I'm Kind of a Big Deal

In 1954 Marilyn Monroe was probably the most famous person alive.

She was in her late twenties and had been performing in some of Hollywood's biggest movies. Characterized by her beauty and enigmatic star status, she managed to draw crowds anywhere she went. In a sense, Monroe was perhaps the first superstar celebrity, to keep their cool while millions lost their minds at the mere sight of her. Long story short, Marilyn Monroe was a big deal.

In 1954, Monroe was in Los Angeles, at a small unnamed jazz club taking in the night's entertainment. Inevitably she'd been followed to the venue by a throng of journalists and paparazzi photographers. She'd walked through the venue with all eyes on her, and she'd taken her seat without one person looking at the stage. With a carefully cultivated public image, Monroe knew how to keep up appearances, but also appreciated music. Given her difficult personal life, it's not difficult to understand why. Music was probably one of the few things that Monroe could absorb and enjoy, knowing that it hadn't been put on just for her and that the act was genuine, not for celebrities. From her seat, she watched a larger-than-life jazz singer take to the stage and sing some of the most beautiful music she had ever heard.

That singer, Ella Fitzgerald, is now dubbed "the Queen of Jazz" and the "First Lady of Song." Fitzgerald found success in the 1940s and 1950s through tours, where she took her chance to sing across America and even Australia. She turned to a solo career in jazz, produced by legendary jazz producer and promoter Norman Granz, in the mid-1940s. However, despite her success, being a Black woman in those times was difficult, and Ella experienced racial discrimination while on tour.

In her own words, Ella explained her experiences:

> *"I know I make a lot of money at the jazz clubs I play, but I sure wish I could play at one of those fancy places."*

Ella was undeniably successful on the jazz circuit by 1954, already seen as a celebrated vocal virtuoso. When Marilyn Monroe saw her at the small club, she went to meet the exceptional singer afterwards and they quickly became friends. Her voice was incredible - for sure one of the best around - and Marilyn asked her why she wasn't performing at the Mocambo in Hollywood, a successful nightclub that Monroe particularly loved.

The truth was that Granz had attempted to get Ella Fitzgerald into the Mocambo before but had failed to do so. Some decades later, the story emerged that Fitzgerald was refused playtime at the Mocambo because of her race, which she denied as the truth. The stage at the Mocambo was very commonly populated with musicians of all races; their treatment off stage was where all sense of equality ended, however. The manager of the Mocambo had been quite blunt that Ella Fitzgerald simply didn't have enough glamour or sex appeal to warrant putting her on stage there.

Though hardly out of shape, Ella Fitzgerald wasn't the stereotypical vision of show business in the 1950s. That was more…, well, that was Marilyn Monroe's deal. Monroe felt that Ella had been unfairly held back from stardom. She was unhappy to hear of Ella's failure to grace her favorite stage, so decided to speak to the manager of the Mocambo herself.

Monroe convinced the manager to hire Fitzgerald for a full week in 1955. The man was initially unsure, but when Marilyn Monroe said that she'd be in the front row of the club every single night for that week, all was agreed upon. He knew that if Monroe was there, then every seat would be sold out, the press would be banging at the door, and all of Hollywood would be speaking about the Mocambo!

Jet magazine reported of Fitzgerald that fateful week: "(she has) smooth vocals which lured some of the biggest singing names in show business."

Ella didn't play the small clubs after that; she didn't have to. She now had the Mocambo on her resume, which she played often during the rest of her career. With a huge club like that on the record, the small clubs just didn't compare.

Ella Fitzgerald died in 1996, as one of the world's most recognized and loved singers. She publicly spoke of Monroe's generosity in boosting her career and felt that the face of Hollywood was decades ahead of her time - looking after women regardless of the societal boundaries put up by others around her.

Just Dig Down, How Hard Can It Be?

Have you heard of flat-earthers? You might say, "They think the Earth is flat? How!? *Everyone* knows the Earth is round!" In fact, it has been proved as round repeatedly, but for some reason, there is still a sect of the human population who simply don't believe it.

Not only that but for a time, there was a similar style of belief known as the Hollow Earth theory, which even achieved the stamp of approval from the President of the United States!

From 1825–29, the sixth president, a man called John Quincy Adams, had command of the United States of America, the world's newest great democracy. Adams had been a top student at Harvard University, which was even in America's infancy recognized as a world-leading education institute. He became the world's greatest diplomat, helped free enslaved people accused of mutiny, and was the first president to be interviewed by a woman. In short, for a powerful man at the start of the 19th century, he was multifaceted and probably a bit more forward-thinking than many of his contemporaries.

And yet…, he also believed the world was hollow and filled with other subterranean worlds!

The Hollow Earth theory had been around for a while and was first conceptualized, as far as we know, in the 17th century. The idea of a hollow Earth, or something like that, first emerged in ancient mythology and was then developed during the intellectual debates of the late 1600s. While medicine was advancing, the world was being discovered, and science was experiencing fast improvements, so every bit of knowledge was up for grabs.

One of the big questions was "What does the inside of the Earth look like?" When you think about it, it's a difficult question. How could people with limited geological knowledge be sure? Suggested answers included a series of tubes and water pipes that connect the North and South poles, and a series of shells, like a Russian doll, that have their own separate poles and rotations. The Hollow Earth theory was discredited quite definitively by a scientist from the Royal Society called Charles Hutton in 1774. He conducted an experiment that's far too complicated for this book, but let's just say it determined that the Earth could not be hollow and must be rock all the way through.

If we know anything about conclusive scientific theories, however, it is that there's always someone somewhere who thinks that the theory is wrong. That person in our story is John Cleves Symmes Jr., an army officer and lecturer who became obsessed with the Hollow Earth theory.

Symmes believed there was a way to access the inner Earth, through large holes found at the North and South poles. It's worth mentioning that there are no such holes, but this wasn't known in 1820 when Symmes broadcast his theory. No expedition had made its way to the South Pole yet, and wouldn't until 1911, so why wouldn't there be holes there?

Symmes was convinced that there were beings inside the Earth - and who knows what they'd be like? He decided that leading an expedition to the Earth was the only way to find out what lay inside. He published a pamphlet, seeking 100 "brave companions" to join him on a mission to the North Pole, led across the frozen sea of Siberia by reindeer.

Symmes wasn't wealthy enough to pay 100 men, nor their 100 or so reindeer, so he sought help from the president, John Quincy Adams. Adams was taken by the theory and was convinced of its scientific and global importance. He agreed to fund the full expedition from the public purse. Unfortunately for Symmes, he had asked Adams about a year too late.

Their conversation was in 1829, and that year Adams was voted out of the presidential office in favor of Andrew Jackson who, for some reason, scrapped the expedition almost immediately. Symmes died shortly after Jackson's inauguration and never got a chance to meet the mole-like creatures he envisaged hidden in the Earth's core.

The Hollow Earth theory largely petered out after this bizarre story, with most satisfied that the Earth is not hollow, and you shouldn't try to find out if it is, because you'll melt to death. The theory is still popular with writers, spawning a few books and even a terrible movie about the concept.

You'll Do Anything
to Stop Being "Board"

America is a country full of avid entertainment consumers, which has always been the case. TV and movies dominate discussions at work, while musicians are hailed as otherworldly gods, capable of turning on the tap of emotion with a few simple notes. One form of fun in America, the well of which has never run dry, is the board game industry.

The board game market is huge and is currently going through something of a revival. Now worth a staggering $17 billion, almost all people will have played a board game at some point, be it Monopoly, Chess, Scrabble, Clue, Trivial Pursuit, or the focus of our story, Candyland.

Candyland has remained popular in the US since its creation in the 1940s, currently selling at least one million copies every year. The game is simple by design:

1. Players race down a linear track, with each space colored one of six colors, some of which have special candy symbols.

2. They draw from a deck of cards that matches the board's colors or symbols.
3. The player moves the token to the next space matching the color on the card or teleports to the space matching the symbol.
4. The player that first reaches the end, wins.

It's a very basic game and is aimed at young children. Players don't have to be skilled at anything to win, there's no conceptual understanding required, and the element of chance keeps families guessing at who's going to take first place. If you're reading this and are thinking, "I hate Candy Land, I truly, truly do," then you won't be surprised to learn that studies suggest parents despise playing the game, while their kids love it.

Its success lies in the mind of its creator, Eleanor Abbott. Abbott was a schoolteacher, suffering from polio during a particularly nasty epidemic in the 1940s and 1950s. In the modern world, polio is almost entirely eradicated due to the successful rollouts of vaccinations in the 20th century, but in the 1940s, it was serious business and could lead to irreversible paralysis.

Abbott was in a polio ward in San Diego, California, receiving treatment and battling through sickness. She observed that children were being confined due to the illness, both inside the ward and out of it. Patients were hooked up to machinery and medical equipment, while non-sufferers were kept inside by nervous parents to avoid catching polio. Abbott, knowledgeable as she was about children and how they think, devised Candy Land for the children in her ward.

The kids loved the game and parents enjoyed playing it together; it helped transport them to somewhere beyond the hospital walls. It was essentially a gift for these families.

Mel Taft, an executive at Milton Bradley (MB), a major board game company who brought such titles as Yahtzee, Connect Four, and Twister to household tables (and floors) went to visit Abbott once she'd recovered.

Abbott displayed a simple design drawn on some butcher paper. Taft was quite charmed by Abbott and felt that her game came from an innocent place and that her insight into children, as a teacher, was worth paying attention to.

What we know after this point is vague, but MB began to produce the game, and Abbott was paid something for her role as its creator.

Abbott donated the money that she received over the next 40 years of her life to children in need. The game is ranked in the top ten-selling board games of all time, with at least 50 million copies sold. Its creation speaks volumes about Abbott's dedication to children and her desire to see them happy.

Polio, Polio, Away You Go-lio

If there's anything to be learned from medical advancement in the 20th century, it's that it's a moneymaker. The health sector can make a vast amount of money for industry leaders and company directors because it offers something that is very often unavailable anywhere else. Until recently, in the US, insulin (a common and necessary drug for diabetic patients to have access to) could regularly cost $300. In February 2023, Eli Lilly (a company that manufactures insulin) announced that they would cut costs for customers to $35, which still means that the company makes back more than *three times* what it spends to make it - and they were heavily praised for their generosity!

Some countries across the world have access to universal healthcare, such as the United Kingdom, Canada, Germany, and Japan. The citizens of these countries have access to life-saving healthcare for no payment beyond their tax money and a standardized cost for prescription medication. The money in big pharmaceutical business empires is made away from the public's eye, regardless of how much they pay at the checkout. The drugs, medication, and equipment are all produced by companies that want to see a return on their investment. The scientists and companies who make the medication stand to make an inordinate amount of money by making the drug *first* and then patenting it.

In 1955, a man called Jonas Salk stood on the precipice of being a multi-millionaire, if not a billionaire, for creating an effective polio vaccine..., and he decided to turn down that opportunity.

Salk was born in 1914 in New York City, to a working-class, immigrant family. He had an aptitude for science and medicine from a young age and went on to become a doctor by 25. During World War II, Salk helped to develop an influenza vaccine that was used to protect the armed forces from illness. As the war came to a close, Salk was an established scientist with a background in creating effective vaccines. The University of Pittsburgh rewarded him with control of a lab of his own at the School of Medicine. He decided to devote his life to finding a vaccine for polio.

Salk spent the first year gathering researchers and other scientists to join his team and started experimenting. Another scientist, Albert Sabin, was working on an oral vaccine using strains of the disease that were alive, something that Salk saw as being dangerous and likely to lead to failure. He decided that using a dead strain would be safer and yield better results.

It's important to remember that polio was a deadly illness that had high incidence numbers. In 1952, 21,000 people were paralyzed due to the disease in America alone. The immensely popular United States President Franklin D. Roosevelt contracted the disease in 1945. Unsurprisingly, the world was terrified of polio, and support for a cure was high. The funding poured in for Salk. In all, by 1955, $67 million had been donated to the project.

Salk began testing his vaccine on children, and by 1954, almost one million children had formed a group known as the "polio pioneers." They were part of a wave of mass testing to ensure that the vaccine would work across a large cross-section of people. It proved successful and the vaccine was announced as safe in 1955.

Vaccination campaigns were rolled out and the mass production process for the potentially life-saving drug rumbled into action. Today, polio is all but eradicated, with only one strain remaining active globally.

With such a successful vaccination, Salk stood to make a vast sum of money. In fact, modern estimates put the value of the vaccination at approximately $7 billion. However, Salk decided not to patent his vaccine, due to his moral convictions. He was staunch in his belief that the vaccine should be available to everyone and not protected by some copyright to guarantee his fortune. When he was asked on TV who owns the patent to his lifesaving work, he responded:

> *"Well, the people I would say. There is no patent. Could you patent the sun?"*

The good doctor went on to found the Salk Institute for Biological Studies in California in 1960 and continued his research into virology and immunology until he died in 1995. Salk was the recipient of several awards in his life including the Presidential Medal of Freedom, but his humble attitude toward his groundbreaking work is what stands out. His refusal to take the money, in the full knowledge that it would have assured his family's life for many generations, because he saw the bigger picture, is truly inspiring.

Fighting on Arrival, Fighting for Survival

If you were paying attention to the singles charts in 1983 (if you were alive) then you'd have seen, in the last week of July, a now-famous song called 'Buffalo Soldier' reach number one. The song was recorded by the globally successful reggae artist Bob Marley in 1978 and had been released in 1983, two years after his death. It's become one of his most well-received songs and many will recognize it from simply singing the words "buffalo soldier," in the way it's put in the song.

The story behind is based on American history that is often overlooked. Marley's track brought some attention to it, reframing the narrative as part of the continuous fight for civil rights in America that had been a dominant part of American politics for decades.

The Buffalo Soldiers was a name given to several units of all-Black soldiers, created after the end of the American Civil War (1861–65). The Civil War had been fought, in part, over slavery. Slavery had been a dominant economic contributor in the United States of America, and the country was divided on whether to abandon the trade. Due to that and ensuring political disagreements, the country went to war with itself. The Black soldiers who fought for the victorious Unionist side were, in a sense, fighting for their own freedom.

As the war ended and the country began work on repairing and healing after years of conflict, many Black citizens were keen on signing up to fight for the army. The pay was low at approximately $13 per month but was more than most Black Americans could hope to earn in the mid-19th century. Black Americans also saw the army as a respectable form of work, where they would receive better treatment than they would in most forms of employment.

In 1866, Congress established six units of all-Black soldiers, fighting in the West against Native Americans. It was here that they gained the Buffalo Soldiers nickname, which was given to them by the Native Americans. The latter distinguished the all-Black units from the White units by their hair, noting their black and curly hair as distinctive from those of White people. Native Americans also had respect for the units' ferocity and tenacity in battle.

The Plains Indians, who had been embroiled in conflict with the US government, gave the units the nickname based on those two traits: 1) hair that is like a buffalo's and 2) energy and tenacity like a buffalo.

The nickname stuck and the Buffalo Soldiers became something of a staple of the US Army. Soldiers from the unit served as the first caretakers of national parks such as Yosemite and Sequoia. The units fought wildfires, prosecuted poachers, constructed roads, stopped illegal use of the land, and performed other jobs that we would now associate with a ranger.

The distinguished troops were a permanent fixture in the US Army for almost 90 years, serving until the Korean War in the 1950s, after which they were disbanded and segregated units were ended. Their story is better known for Bob Marley's song, an interesting tale of a very disenfranchised people who had suffered for centuries in America but found employment fighting for its sanctity and security.

The Ever-So Beautiful Game

Let's get one thing straight, right at the start of this story. The game commonly known as "soccer" by Americans is referred to as "football" by approximately 90% of the world - where it's a much more popular sport than other "football" codes!

Still, even if you're an American soccer fan, you may be aware of the name Didier Drogba. Drogba is now retired but was a world-class talent from the Cote d'Ivoire (Aka. the Ivory Coast) who played at the highest level of soccer for approximately a decade. Signed by English Premier League super team Chelsea in 2004, Drogba cemented his name as a legend at the London club and was part of Cote D'Ivoire's "golden generation" of footballers.

Inherently, a story about sportsmen being overpaid for their work isn't interesting or uplifting, but Didier Drogba's career entered a strange arena in 2005. His career had lifted into the stratosphere, as he scored a decent number of goals in his first season at Chelsea and had started his second season well when there was a break for international games that would decide qualification for the World Cup.

Cote d'Ivoire had, at this time, never competed in the World Cup, but now they had a chance. Their team had to win their game against Sudan, one which should be easy, and Cameroon had to lose or draw their game against Egypt. This was a huge sporting occasion for Cote d'Ivoire's population, who were set to witness history. However, there were bigger things on the citizens' minds...

In 2002, Cote d'Ivoire erupted into civil war as government forces faced off against the New Forces of Ivory Coast. As is often the case in civil conflict, the situation is complicated and requires more delicate reading than this small story can offer. What is important to acknowledge is that violence was widespread, there were approximately 3,000 casualties, and the UN had to take military action.

October 8, 2005, now three years into the conflict, Cote d'Ivoire came through and beat Sudan as expected. The stadium remained full as the game ended, with the players standing in the center, waiting for news from the Cameroon-Egypt fixture that would determine their World Cup involvement. Right at the last second, Cameroon was awarded a penalty which, if scored, would bring them victory and send Cote d'Ivoire crashing out of contention for the World Cup!

Everyone left in the stadium groaned. To come this close and fail seemed beyond cruel. Radios were tuned in, and the team strained their ears in the center of the pitch. Drogba was among them, listening to the last few seconds.

Cameroon missed!

An eruption of joyous exultation burst from the stadium. Cote d'Ivoire would be going to their first-ever World Cup, with the best team they've ever had. It didn't matter how far they went; the fact that they competed was enough. The team took to their dressing room to celebrate, and a TV camera rushed in to interview the team. Meeting them was the big Chelsea man himself, Didier Drogba, microphone in hand. He said:

"Men and women of Ivory Coast. From the north, south, center, and west, we proved today that all Ivorians can coexist and play together with a

119

shared aim - to qualify for the World Cup. We promised you that the celebrations would unite the people - today we beg you on our knees."

The players, at this point, all sunk to their knees. Drogba continued:

"The one country in Africa with so many riches must not descend into war. Please lay down your weapons and hold elections."

Over the next weeks and months, Drogba's statement was replayed on televisions across Cote d'Ivoire repeatedly, as if it might inspire peace into happening. It seemed to have some effect. Slowly, the two sides moved closer to peace discussions, and a ceasefire was signed, with Drogba's message of cooperation being the backdrop to the movement toward peace.

The country has limped on since but is in a greater state of peace than previously. The country's national soccer team had a decent showing over the next decade, but ultimately, making a joint statement of peace is probably the most important thing that the team achieved.

BLYthely Setting the Standards for Investigative Journalism

If you possess even a cursory knowledge of the late 1800s, you may be aware that times were rather difficult for women. In most countries, women weren't granted the right to vote and often didn't even have the right to own their own land. It was at the turning of the 20th century that the women's suffrage movements gained momentum and the tide turned gradually, ensuring that women had more agency over their lives.

However, people can be remarkably persistent, especially when they're being persecuted. Introducing Nellie Bly.

Nellie Bly (real name Elizabeth Jane Cochran) was born in Pennsylvania, USA in 1864. Her childhood was marked by a dad who fathered 13 daughters and a lack of funds to keep her in education. Elizabeth was intelligent, however, and a voracious reader. She regularly engaged herself with local news and was dismayed to read, in 1885, an article in the *Pittsburgh Dispatch* that stated women were principally on the Earth to birth babies and tidy the house. Unfortunately, that was not an uncommon opinion at the time.

Elizabeth wrote into the dispatch under the pseudonym of "Lonely Orphan Girl," criticizing the article. In doing so she gained the attention of the editor, George Madden. Madden hired Cochran to write several articles, leading her to adopt her lasting pseudonym, Nellie Bly. She wrote of the hardships of being a woman, the need for divorce reform, and the right for women to work and be independent. Though the opinions were undoubtedly against the grain for some, Nellie was writing during the emergence of what we could consider the first women's rights movement, and her writing became popular and zeitgeisty.

Nellie went on to set the standard for investigative journalism through two notable stunts. She is well known for setting the first world record in 1888 for completing the journey undertaken by Phileas Fogg in 'Around the World in Eighty Days', in 72 days. Her write-up in book form was loved, and she gained great attention, though she didn't keep the record for long. Her truly remarkable achievement, though was her exposé about asylums, completed in 1887.

"Mental asylums" as they were often referred to in the 19th century, were barbaric places. Far before awareness about mental health problems and illness, people who were suffering from these issues both curable and severe were removed from society and placed in asylums. Modern knowledge tells us that an asylum does very little to improve anyone's mental health, and the institutions were often home to bizarre experiments and prison-like treatment.

Bly had secured employment at *New York World*, a popular paper circulating in the Big Apple at the time and agreed to go undercover at the Women's Lunatic Asylum on Blackwell's (now Roosevelt's) Island. Bly feigned mental illness by causing panic in a boarding house, where she frightened lodgers with threats and bizarre behavior. The police took her away, and she was taken to Blackwell's Island after an examination by a doctor, judge, and police officer (not in that order).

What followed was a ten-day stint at the institution, during which time Bly experienced the barbarity of the asylum for herself. She instantly dropped the act of insanity once inside, but the staff didn't seem to notice. Their vision of the world, blurred by the bizarre location of their work, had rendered them unable to see even typical behavior as anything but "insane." Bly's actions were noted by nurses as evidence of her insanity, when she was doing perfectly normal things like walking around, talking politely, and using the facilities as intended.

Bly reported nurses beating patients, as well as abusive language, rotten food, and undrinkable water. She documented patients being tied together, while rats and human waste were a constant presence in the eating hall. At the end of the ten days, *New York World* demanded her release, and she was extracted from the institution. Her subsequent report and book, entitled *Ten Days in a Mad-House*, was a sensation.

'Ten Days in a Mad-House' led to a widespread change of practice in asylums, particularly in terms of the treatment of women. Bly was scathing in her report and publicly shamed the poor practice on constant display. Her legacy lasted longer than the immediate reform as well.

Today, mental asylums have been replaced with actual medical facilities that care for those with serious mental illness.

The vision Bly provided of abuse, neglect, and bullying tainted the image of a 19th-century institution, undoubtedly affecting our media since. Movies featuring asylums such as *'Shutter Island'* and *'One Flew Over the Cuckoo's Nest'* were both hits upon release. The popular television series *'American Horror Story'* loosely based a full season on Bly's time at the asylum, and other movies and stage adaptations have been created from her book.

Bly's work changed the perception of the female journalist. The stuntwoman journalism that followed her career is a testament to the changing image of women all over America. Bly was not content with the small pittances that she was provided with, journalism-wise, and crafted a new genre of investigative journalism that has contributed greatly to leveling the playing field between genders.

He was Probably Quite a Smug Child

Will child prodigies ever *stop* being interesting? About once a year, every media outlet will run a story (normally on a slow news day) about a young child who is far, far cleverer than all other children and far, far better at one skill. We teach our kids, quite rightly, that they're all unique and are all special in their own way. However, we humans do like to point at one particular child and shout, "That one is the best though!"

Arguably, the whole obsession with finding a child prodigy/genius started far in the past. No, not with the movie *Good Will Hunting* but with a child born in Salzburg, Austria in 1756. His name was Wolfgang Amadeus Mozart, and he would go on to become one of the most prolific classical composers of all time, with an impressive 800+ compositions to his name.

Wolfgang was born to a father who was himself a relatively successful musician, playing fourth violin at one of the royal households of

Salzburg. As an educator and trained musician, he was keen to impart a love for music to his children. Unfortunately for Leopold and his wife Anna Maria, five of their seven children died in infancy, a startling fact, though infant mortality was very high in the 18th century, so it was not unheard of at the time. Still, Leopold started teaching his daughter, Nannerl, how to play the keyboard at the age of seven, while his three-year-old son watched on.

Nannerl was a good musician, but she later recalled how her brother seemed to understand the formation of music amazingly well for his age. Leopold decided that he may as well begin educating the child at four years old, as he seemed to have something of a knack for it. Nannerl recalled this moment later in her life:

"In the fourth year of his age his father, for a game as it were, began to teach him a few minuets and pieces at the clavier (keyboard). He could play it faultlessly and with the greatest delicacy, and keeping exactly in time…."

We aren't totally sure when Mozart began composing, but we have an estimate. It was sometime between his fourth and sixth birthdays. The young child started by composing *K. 1-5*, a few short compositions, approximately 30 seconds long each. If you find some time, YouTube them. They're simple, and if they were composed by an adult, you'd probably give a wry smile and think, "Well, they're okay at the piano." But for a child of that age, they're remarkable. Wolfgang Amadeus Mozart was clearly gifted, and his father quickly recognized that he'd need better teaching than he was capable of giving.

Both Wolfgang and his sister traveled Europe as child prodigies during the 1760s and early 70s. They journeyed to Germany, England, Netherlands, Switzerland, and France, enjoying the delights of fame as mere children. Wolfgang met dozens of the best musicians and composers in Europe at the time, including Johann Sebastian Bach. He heard innovative music and learned complicated techniques quickly - so quickly, in fact, that he was able to compose his first symphony, *Symphony No.1 in Eb*, in 1764 at eight years old. It was scored for two oboes, two horns, and strings.

For the sake of brevity, we'll breeze through Mozart's astonishing career quickly. There's a wealth of information to digest, and it's worth researching it further, but here's an outline:

- He finished his European travel with his sister in 1773, having written several operas and vastly more symphonies. He was 17.
- He was then employed in the royal court at Salzburg, as a court musician. While working there, he composed elegant violin concertos (not his favorite) and expanded his work to new genres of classical music. He grew tired of the position, Salzburg, and the low pay, so left in 1777 and ended up in Paris.
- Living as a struggling musician, Mozart was reduced to pawning off valuables to make ends meet. He was well known, but he didn't want to take just any job; he needed something fulfilling and of the status he felt he deserved. In Paris, he composed continuously, creating the *A Minor Piano Sonata* and the *"Paris" Symphony*.
- In 1779, he moved back to Salzburg, to take up a job, though he still resented the place. He was being paid three times as much as

the last time he'd been there but left again in 1781.

- Mozart premiered an opera called *Idomeneo*, to great success. He was summoned to Vienna, to be with his employer, Archbishop Colloredo, who loved Mozart and valued his ability. However, Mozart left the Archbishop to go and work for the Emperor of the Austrian empire, after impressing him by "whip[ing] through my opera for him and then play[ing] a fugue or two."

- Through the 1780s, Mozart was at his best. He married and had children (though several died) and produced his most famous work including his most famous operas, string quartets, chamber music, and concertos.

- By the mid-1780s, Mozart's lavish lifestyle had plunged him into debt and his health was beginning to fail him. His family struggled with him, though he was the most famous composer of his time, with a certain Ludwig Van Beethoven traveling to Vienna to study under him.

- In 1791, Mozart died at the age of 35. He was composing right until the last moment, producing his celebrated opera *The Magic Flute*. He conducted the music at its premiere. His death was attributed to a mixture of illnesses that were both short- and long-term. When it came to his death, he was in great pain and suffered for weeks.

Mozart had managed to cram a 31-year-long career into a short life and left more than 800 compositions behind. Musicians are rarely able to create so much musical content, and it's baffling to consider how much *more* he could have created had his health been better. Mozart defines "classical music" to many people, and though he died early, his work will continue to outlive generations.

PART THREE:
"...SOMETHING TO HOPE FOR..."

Now onto our third section, which is about hope. In this chapter, you'll read stories that are a bit about the future, or at least are about being hopeful for the future. Included are tales of extraordinary scientific progress, pioneering individuals, and communities coming together for the greater good. We often hear about how the world is doomed, so occasionally it's healthy to take in what good is happening all around us.

Not Everything is For Sale

Witnessing the triumph of the underdog always stirs a profound sense of inspiration within us. That's true whether it's an individual or a small collective boldly advocating for justice, personal liberties, or simply taking a stand when no one else will. It evokes iconic imagery like that of The Tank Man, a poignant 1989 photograph capturing a lone protester in China courageously obstructing a procession of imposing tanks, momentarily disrupting their advance toward quashing a student uprising - a singular frame imbued with defiance and unwavering resolve.

In 2019, the Ecuadorian government found itself ensnared in a similar narrative of unwavering determination, but on the opposing side, as it confronted the indigenous Waorani communities dwelling within the lush bosom of the Amazon Rainforest in Ecuador.

The government's audacious plan was to auction off seven million acres of rainforest to energy companies for oil exploration rights.

Ecuador, shackled by slow economic growth and debt, saw this as a potential lifeline, a way to start breaking down its wall of financial problems. However, for the indigenous communities nestled within this verdant expanse, this proposal spelled the destruction of their ancestral homes and environmental devastation.

In response, the Waorani people took the government to court. The rainforest is home to dozens of communities whose lives would be uprooted by the destruction of the natural surroundings in favor of oil extraction. Plus, the environmental impact of clearing such a vast amount of the world's largest rainforest would be dire. The court found in the indigenous people's favor, ruling that the sale of the land without their consent would be illegal.

The victory of the Waorani community stands as a resounding testament to indigenous rights, a milestone for those dwelling within the Amazon rainforest, a region relentlessly assailed by deforestation over the past century. In Puyo and far beyond, jubilant Waorani members poured into the streets to celebrate the court's historic decision.

However, the Ecuadorian government remains undeterred, and it is intent on appealing the verdict through different legal avenues. The Waorani people have made it equally clear that they will carry their cause to the highest level of international courts before giving up their lands to greed. In this David-and-Goliath-style epic, the spirit of resilience and justice endures as a beacon of hope.

I.O.U. a Life-Saving Amount of Money

Ireland has had a connection to America for generations. Some of the first migrants and settlers to the country were from Ireland, and areas such as Boston and Scituate have a large population of American Irish people. However, Ireland's connection to the people of America doesn't start and end with White settlers. In the 19th century, Ireland struck up an unexpected but welcome relationship with the Choctaw Nation, a Native American territory consisting of several tribes.

The Choctaw Nation saw themselves as similar to Ireland in many ways. Leaders highlighted Ireland's struggle against the English throughout history including resisting genocide, fighting for sovereignty, and experiencing the horrors of colonization. The Nation pointed out that these crimes were levied against the Native Americans as well. With their native languages being discouraged and local customs dissuaded, the Choctaw Nation proudly saw themselves as being like Ireland, with similar struggles.

It was this relationship, or perhaps the Nation's ability to acknowledge another group's suffering, that led them to try to help Ireland in 1847. Throughout the 1840s, Ireland was suffering from the Potato Famine, which was a blight that prevented much crop growth in Ireland and caused the death of around one million people. In modern times, it's forgotten how serious this event was. Thousands were displaced or forced to emigrate to England and America to escape the famine.

The Choctaw Nation had had a difficult decade as well. By 1847, they'd been forced onto a reservation, something that Native Americans were plainly against but had little agency to prevent. They settled in southeast Oklahoma, where they are to this day, on a mighty area of land that is bigger than some states. They had heard of the famine in Ireland and quickly organized a donation of $5,000 to send to help. The money went to one specific town called Midleton in County Cork, which would go on for a few decades before realizing where the crucial funds had come from.

It took until the 1990s for proper recognition of the Choctaw's selfless act to occur. The leaders of the Nation visited County Mayo to take part in the Famine Walk to honor the victims of the blight. Since then, Ireland has honored the Choctaw Nation in several ways, including:

- A plaque in the Lord Mayor of Dublin's house installed in 1992.
- Irish President Mary Robinson visited the Nation's headquarters in 1995 to formally thank them for their generosity.
- A sculpture called Kindred Spirits was erected in a park in Midleton, County Cork, to honor the donation.

Most remarkable of all was how, in 2020, Ireland was able to give something back to people who had helped them almost two centuries before. As the COVID-19 pandemic surged onward, the Choctaw Nation was hit hard, through the loss of life and other social impacts. News reached Ireland that the Choctaw Nation was struggling greatly with the effects of the virus, so a GoFundMe was set up to help and to "pay something forward."

The GoFundMe page is still active as of September 2023 and has taken in more than $8 million, which goes toward charitable help for the Choctaw Nation and other Native American tribes. In the early days of its creation, there was an almost overwhelming amount of financial support from Irish people who were more than happy to help. It's quite wonderful to see activism and assistance develop between two groups of people that many would assume are quite separate nations.

Let There Be Light! And Ideally - a Television Next

Despite centuries of development, 1.1 billion people live without access to power. Disproportionately, this affects people in Low-Income Countries who are unable to effectively utilize the nighttime in the same way that more privileged countries can.

For this 1.1 billion, when the sun sets in the evening, they are in the dark. Work and learning cease, and there are not many options in most places but to sleep. In most communities where there is no available power, the choice is to use lamps that burn fuel such as kerosene. which emits harmful levels of air pollution. This negatively affects the fight against climate change as well as harms the users. A lot of work needs to be done to bring these communities power, and ideally, it should be done without causing greater harm to our planet.

Luckily, there are some solutions. Solar power has become one of the world's more dominant power sources after fossil fuels. Solar power is nothing new; its history traces back almost 70 years, and solar panels have been in use for much of the 21st century. It seems both sensible and useful to provide solar power where possible, especially if starting from scratch.

This is the logic that Barefoot College employs. The college is an international, woman-centered, global network that works to develop rural communities. They currently operate in over 90 countries and their work is bringing great success to areas that would have little to no chance without them.

The college runs a six-month training program where women are trained in how to install and maintain solar panels and lamps, which bring electricity and light to communities. The course also educates women in other areas such as financial management, health education, reproductive health, and the use of technology in their day-to-day lives. The work helps empower women in rural, poor communities, who are disadvantaged in finding work outside the home.

The college has received funding from a variety of donors, such as UN Women, Coca-Cola, and

Hogan Lovells, to keep the programs running and hopefully work on expansion. The empowerment being gifted to women by the college through education is helping power their world for the future.

Florentina Choc, from Belize, had this to say about the program:

> "*In my village, there are 68 households. All the panels and lights for these homes, I installed… Once I brought light to my community, I could see it. Something changed in the village, not like before when we stayed in the dark. Now my village has light.*"

Empowering societies to work for their future is important, and Barefoot College helps make this achievable. Having poor access to power has such a negative effect when our world is as interconnected as it is. After all, there's some discussion around access to the internet being a human right in the modern world. Hopefully, with more work like the College is doing, there'll be a not-too-distant end to communities being without power, and the world can develop and move forward together.

Are You Ever Going to Come Down From There?

If you find the very idea of a protest annoying, disruptive, and ruinous, then you may not necessarily enjoy this story. However, it is remarkable and helps us see that we humans are aware of our future and that it is in jeopardy.

Here we're focusing on Julia Lorraine Hill, who was born in 1974 to a family that was constantly on the move. Her father was a traveling minister, whose job necessitated town-to-town travel, and his family was brought along with him. This meant that, for Julia, her childhood was spent living in a campervan as part of a five-person family.

The claustrophobia of such a small living environment compelled Julia to explore the outdoors as much as possible. She took long hikes, explored national parks, and particularly adored rivers. At seven years old, while on such an exploration with her family, a butterfly landed on her finger and remained for the duration of the hike. From then, she gained the nickname "Butterfly."

Julia's family eventually settled when she was reaching the double-digits, and she attended middle school in Jonesboro, Arkansas. The next decade or so of Julia's life was relatively "normal" but unfulfilling. Julia had lost touch with the natural wonder that she'd had as a child like so many of us do. Leaving school at 16 and working in hospitality, she later remarked:

"I had been obsessed with my career, success, and material things."

In 1996, at the age of 22, Julia was almost killed in a horrific car accident. She had been the designated driver, taking her friend home from a night out, when a drunk driver crashed into the back of her car. Julia hit her head hard against the steering wheel, causing it to penetrate her skull.

Julia was unable to speak or move after the accident, but through the wonders of modern medicine and a year's worth of intensive therapy, she was able to walk and talk again. Everything was not back to normal, however; something had inexorably changed within Julia.

"I realized that my whole life had been out of balance… the crash woke me up to the importance of the moment, and doing whatever I could to make a positive impact on the future."

In 1996, Julia undertook a bit of soul searching, which is not unusual for people who have gone through a life-changing event. She had been questioning her career and felt it was pointless to simply go back to her life.

She found her way to California and ended up with a group who were protesting the removal of old Redwood trees that overlooked the community of Stafford, south of Scotia. The group was angry at the indiscriminate removal of the aged, colossal trees, and further angry at the destruction of houses in Stafford, caused by landslides. They needed someone to stay in a tree for a week, to send a message, and to render the site unsafe for continued logging.

Guess who put their hand up?

On 10 December 1997, Julia was strapped into a harness, ready to ascend a 1,000-year-old tree that stood at 180 feet high. She wasn't a member of any environmental organization, but she felt compelled to help the local community. Final provisions had been loaded into the tree on two platforms that had been constructed for Julia to live on for the next week. Except it didn't turn out to be a week.

Julia lived in the tree, dubbed Luna, for 738 days. The longer that she was in the tree, the more media coverage the protest received. Radio stations phoned her for interviews and TV news anchors arrived to cover the developing story. She weathered freezing winds and a barrage of harassment from security guards and angry loggers.

In 1999, the lumber company reached an agreement with the activists to protect Luna and all trees within a 200-foot buffer zone. Julia would leave the tree, and donations were to be made to Humboldt State University, which was conducting research into sustainable forestry and logging.

Hill has continued to advocate for sustainable human living and climate activism. She's become something of a figurehead for the movement, with multiple references to her in music, television, and film. Though protesting is disruptive, it has to be by its very nature. We know now that our actions of the past are damaging our future, so it's through people like Julia "Butterfly" Hill that we can confront our way of living.

All Aboard the Solar Express

Plane travel is arguably the worst travel on the planet. Planes are remarkable pieces of technology, able to transport us over impossible distances in a very short time. The fact that you can go from the UK to Australia in a little over a day is incredible, and perhaps we don't marvel at that enough.

However, the whole business around airlines is a huge polluter. Every day across the world millions of cars drive, using their petrol and diesel engines, to airports to drop passengers off. The passengers then go through huge buildings with thousands of employees, all concerned with the sole purpose of getting the passenger into a giant tube filled with petrol. The planes themselves then rocket into the sky, polluting the atmosphere with their fumes. Airplanes' CO_2 output has increased by about 30% in six years, to almost a billion tons of CO_2. To remain as interconnected as we are, planes are necessary, so how do we make them better for the environment?

A very clever man by the name of Bertrand Piccard has worked on this goal for much of his professional life. In 2016, he proudly demonstrated the potential for solar-powered planes, when he flew one around the world.

The project is called the Solar Impulse, and its last aircraft was the Impulse 2. The plane has a huge wingspan, bigger than a Boeing 747, and more than 17,000 solar cells on its vast wings. For 15 years, Piccard had been working on developing a plane that used renewable energy, and by 2015, he was confident that it could fly around the world. Piccard departed Abu Dhabi in the Impulse 2 on March 15, 2015, and completed a 14,854-mile round trip in 23 days.

Along the way, Piccard stopped in China, California, Spain, Egypt, Myanmar, India, and several cities in the US, to show off the potential behind the technology.

> *"I hope people will understand that it is not just a first in the history of aviation, but also a first in the history of energy."*

The plane was quite slow, traveling at 30 mph, though it could go faster if the sun was bright. Its solar cells made up more than two-thirds of its weight, and the craft suffered difficulties along its journey. However, the team broke the world record for the longest uninterrupted journey in aviation history when completing a 4,000-mile stretch from Japan to Hawaii and made a great statement.

The UN secretary-general was full of praise, commending the team for their ingenuity, and dubbed the event as an "historic day for humanity." The real question is going to be how the technology has progressed from the Solar Impulse. In its current form, it's not suitable for transporting passengers over long distances, but it's a start. If progress is fast enough, the solar power in the impressive craft could help halt the production of hundreds of millions of tons of C02 and will enable us to have fully operational planes that produce no emissions whatsoever.

"You may be ending your around-the-world flight today, but the journey to a more sustainable world is just beginning. The Solar Impulse team is helping to pilot us into that future."

And That's a Hat Trick for Future Prime Minister Rashford!

If we like to do one thing as a society, it's to overpay our entertainers. Our footballers, musicians, and movie stars are provided with over-inflated wages and egos because we love the joy they bring. There's not much that the individual can do about that, but we can hope that the money is used wisely, which it sometimes is, but not often.

In the world of soccer, we see a great many players get paid colossal wages and waste them. It turns out that giving 20-year-olds £5 million per year leads to excessive partying, sports cars, mansions, watches, and all kinds of luxury purchases, leaving very little by the time they're 45. However, for Marcus Rashford, the superstar England and Manchester United player, his desires lie elsewhere.

Rashford came from a poor, single-parent family. His mother, Mel, worked three jobs to provide for five children and Marcus became accustomed to a life of food poverty. Mel was too proud to admit to people that she was struggling to provide for her children, so put herself under extreme stress to secure what she could. From the age of five, Marcus began playing football for a local academy and was touted as a talent early on.

Relying on support from community members and lifts from academy coaches, the five children struggled through childhood until Marcus was given a lifeline at the age of 11. Manchester United asked him to move into club accommodation so that he could train full-time with the club. Since then, Marcus has gone from being a talented youngster to a starter for Manchester United and now earns somewhere around £15 million per year.

Once he began earning serious money, Marcus immediately boosted his family out of poverty, paying for homes for his mother and siblings. However, his upbringing instilled in him a desire to do far more.

"When you come from a place of struggle and pain, a lot of the time it switches and it becomes your drive and motivation."

In March 2020, the United Kingdom went into lockdown due to the global COVID-19 pandemic, and Marcus headed a campaign backed by the charity FareShare, to give meals to vulnerable people. Rashford's campaigning helped to donate almost £20 million to help feed some of the poorer people in the United Kingdom, but his most important work came in June of that year.

The UK provides free school meals to children from poor families, to take financial strain off and provide good, nutritious meals to those pupils who need them. With the COVID-19 lockdown, most of these impoverished families had been temporarily laid off from work and were earning less money. The government announced that, as normal, free school meals would not be provided to children during the six-week summer break during July and August of that year. At the time, 1.3 million children were eligible for free school meals, and they'd been supported by the government until that point. It was a crushing blow for many families.

Marcus openly campaigned to the government, contacting Members of Parliament, to plead with them to reverse their decision. In an emotional and compelling letter, then-23-year-old Rashford spoke of the worsening food poverty in the UK, and how damaging it can be to a young, developing mind. His letters, videos, and public pleas led to further donations to FareShare and, importantly, to the government reversing their decision.

Come September, Rashford had formed a task force of food brands and supermarkets to come up with policy recommendations for the government to fund to help end food poverty:

1. Expand free school meals to reach more children.
2. Expand school holiday food and activities programs.
3. Increase the value of vouchers that help pregnant women and parents with very young children, to reach another 290,000 parents.

The government was again resistant and stated that they didn't have the resources for any such increases to welfare. Once again, Marcus took to the public, starting petitions (gaining millions of signatures), bringing businesses and charities on his side, and personally contacting Prime Minister Boris Johnson to demand greater help for poor families. He was, yet again, successful in his campaign.

Boris Johnson phoned Marcus back to tell him that a £400 million fund had been put together to help provide families with meals and to support families experiencing food poverty. The year 2020 was, all in all, a victory for Rashford, but a greater victory for those poor families who struggled the most during the lockdowns.

In 2021, Marcus was awarded an MBE (Member of the Order of the British Empire) by Prince William due to this work in 2020. His campaigning was admirable, and his refusal to simply accept what had already been given has improved the lives of hundreds of thousands of children across the UK. Providing for poorer people leads to greater social mobility and an improvement in the quality of life for so many people, and hopefully, governments take inspiration from Rashford's continued charity work. With some luck, perhaps more sportspeople will try to emulate it all over the world too.

Swimming, Boxing, and Fighting for Peace

War is never a positive thing. By necessity, someone loses in warfare and too often it's innocent civilians who are the biggest losers. During the 2010s and 2020s, we have seen a huge number of people being displaced, becoming refugees from countries such as Syria, South Sudan, Ethiopia, Afghanistan, and other places that are experiencing conflict.

Refugees are people who have run from their country of origin because of threats to their safety or their lives. Refugees travel through countries, coping with endless bureaucracy, and usually risk their lives doing so. When they eventually reach a place of safety and rest, they're often met with derision or disdain from local populations and struggle to create a life for themselves. It's a desperate situation, and one that no one hopes for, but there have been increasing numbers over the past two decades that have required urgent help.

Helping refugees is complicated. Without a stoppage to war and conflict, people will continue to be displaced and there will be more refugees who need help. But there's always human cooperation and joy to be found around tragedy. In 2016, the Olympic committee made a big step toward ensuring that refugees felt more connected to the wider world and the world of competitive sports.

At the UN General Assembly in October 2015, Thomas Bach, the IOC (International Olympic Committee) President, announced that there would be a Refugee Olympic Team. There had never been a refugee team before, and the announcement was met with intrigue. News outlets, spectators, and athletes alike were all wondering what the impact of a multi-national team would be on the competition.

The team first appeared at the 2016 Olympics in Rio de Janeiro, Brazil to a standing ovation during the opening ceremony. They held the Olympic flag proudly aloft, a symbol of future hope and unity. The team didn't win medals, but their presence was important. With a small team of only ten athletes, their stories became well known and eagerly followed. Understanding that the amazing, world-class athletes were refugees helped bring the humanity of the global crisis back to spectators. Many of the athletes have been compelling advocates for the provision of help and charity for refugees, such as Yusra Mardini, who had a film produced about her in 2022 called *The Swimmers*.

The team also competed in the 2020 Tokyo Olympics (postponed until 2021) with a larger team of 29 athletes from 11 different countries in athletics, boxing, swimming, badminton, Judo, and many other sports, only increasing their visibility. Through the existence of the team, the athletes are acting as ambassadors for the cause of refugees. They're constant reminders of the ongoing refugee crisis and reminders that they are people, with lives, passions, and skills. In an ideal world, the refugee team wouldn't have to exist, but it does, and it forces us to look forward to a time when it won't be necessary anymore.

Bullies Schmullies

We are, all of us, aware that children can be exceptionally cruel. During our years at school, we'd all have seen someone be bullied, been bullied ourselves, or regrettably taken part in the bullying. What's worse is that children maintain that level of cruelty when talking to adults:

"You've put on weight, Dad."

"You're not as funny as you think you are, you know."

"You've gotten really old."

The reason for this, generally, is that children don't understand social graces and norms very well. They think honesty is the best policy, no matter what. Unfortunately, bullying among school children is far more malicious, and intended to hurt. No matter the strategies that are put in place by schools to combat bullying, children across the world experience bullying that can severely affect their happiness for years to come. British pupil Nadia Sparkes, aged 13, experienced the blunt end of this in 2019 when she faced extreme bullying because of her passion for helping her local community.

Nadia's way of helping her community was to leave her house for school one hour early every day so that she had the time to pick up litter before her classes began. She'd also donate her time to do it more often on non-school days, making sure to keep green areas green and litter-free. It's the sort of act that a reasonable adult looks at with a smile, grateful for the volunteered charity from a young teenager. Some would go so far as to say that her actions are inspiring.

Unfortunately, a few pupils at Nadia's high school didn't see it that way, for one reason or another. The bullying that Nadia faced regularly was at times brutal. It started with name-calling, with her classmates dubbing her "Trash Girl." Regrettably, there were few actual friends around Nadia to stand up to this, and the nickname stuck. When bullying occurs, the best time to stop it is near the start of the process, otherwise, it just gets worse, which is what happened to Nadia.

Physical violence began to be enacted, leaving Nadia having to sit through an entire lesson drenched in orange juice that had been poured on her. In an especially serious incident, Nadia was chased and beaten by a pupil brandishing a knife. This last incident was the final straw for Nadia's mother, and the Norfolk police force became involved, with one bully referred to the Youth Offending Team.

As this aggression and bullying reached this new low, Nadia's story gained national attention. Media outlets had picked up on the violent act and had found out about Nadia's charitable acts. Following several online articles and national paper coverage, there was mass online support for Nadia. Many called her a hero for her efforts in her community, and she decided to turn the rude nickname into a positive, saying:

"I'm not going to stop doing the right thing because of them and if they are going to call me trash girl, they can say it with respect. I'm doing something to protect the world they also live in."

Nadia has since found a new school that actively supports her care for the community. She was awarded, along with a green-fingered teacher who champions her, the Points of Light award by then-Prime Minister Theresa May. May wrote to Nadia to express her gratitude to Nadia for being a positive role model for British people to care for their environment.

Nadia continues to volunteer her time to care for the environment, still operating under the name Trash Girl, with a strong online presence that seeks to inspire people to care more about littering and their local environment. Though the circumstances of her recognition are upsetting and should never have come to be, it's fantastic that Nadia exists as a role model and has gained fame despite the bullies' attempts to crush her spirit.

How Happy Are You
on a Scale of 1-10?

Most countries measure their success by economic value. Economists look at the Gross Domestic Product (the value of goods and services) as a universal measure of how well a country is doing. Other measures include examining average household income or unemployment levels. Understandably, we do this; our world is largely dominated by money, and money is required to keep people happy and healthy.

However, in the 1970s, the fourth King of Bhutan, King Jigme Singye Wangchuck proclaimed a different measure of success:

> *"Gross National Happiness is more important than Gross Domestic Product."*

Gross National Happiness is an interesting idea. The King had told the world that the success of Bhutan would be measured by how happy its citizens were. The question of course is: How do you measure someone's happiness? This led to the creation of the Gross National Happiness

(GNH) Index, Bhutan's system of measuring happiness that has been studied and commended by countries across the globe.

The GNH index contains nine domains or sections, which are: Psychological Well-being, Health, Time Use, Education, Cultural Diversity and Resilience, Good Governance, Community Vitality, Ecological Diversity & Resilience, and Living Standards. Within these nine sections are 33 indicators that contribute to what people need for a happy and fulfilled life. The indicators include things such as safety, government performance, spirituality, mental health, work, sleep, education, and more. The GNH index states that if a person has sufficiency in 66% of the indicators, they can be measured as being happy. They then bring all this data in together, combining the happy and not-so-happy people's reports, to decide how happy the whole country is. From this, Bhutan judges where new government policy or welfare programs need to be directed. It's clever but a little bit complicated.

Through data collection and lots of complex mathematics, the government of Bhutan can identify four groups: unhappy, narrowly happy, extensively happy, and deeply happy. Bhutan's government focuses on what makes the deeply happy people so happy and tries to apply what works for them to the unhappy people.

The model has led Bhutan to transition to a democracy, rather than relying solely on the monarchy. It has also led to greater conservation of Bhutan's cultural heritage and of its environment, as a loss of both was seen as a predictor of unhappiness. Throughout the 2020s, Bhutan's people have been reporting greater levels of happiness and the model is being examined by the UN and other governments, who are curious as to what the effects of the model might be.

As our world changes, we may see more countries take this holistic approach to success and development. For example, climate scientists are asking companies to focus less on the production of new products and more on making materials more sustainable and durable. Perhaps as our industry slows down, more governments will measure citizen's happiness, instead of how much money is in their bank accounts.

Coming Soon:
The Hilton at Mars

"Mars. That's the only other planet you could go to in our solar system …Mercury is way too hot, and Venus is horrendously hot with sulfuric acid rain that melts lead on the surface, so you're not going there and the rest of them are made of gas so you're not going there either.

So, Mars is the only place beyond Earth that we could feasibly ever go … we could imagine perhaps going to some of the moons of Jupiter and Saturn in the far future, but that's much more difficult." – Professor Brian Cox, physicist and all-round space nerd.

As we grow older, we have to come to terms with the fact that movies like *'Star Wars'*, television shows such as *'Futurama'*, and books like *'War of the Worlds'* have all promised something that isn't going to happen - alien life in our solar system. Yes, most scientists agree that space holds some sort of other life. It's almost impossible that it doesn't, given its almost infinite possibilities and boundless limits. However, we can be relatively sure that there isn't anything living in our solar system beyond what's already on Earth.

But space is the ultimate in human endeavor. We've explored most of what exists on Planet Earth and are achieving technological heights that we could only have dreamed of 200 years ago. Space exploration and possibly colonization is the next big leap for humanity, should we have the capabilities to do so. After visiting our moon a few times, with India being the latest to do so in 2023, most space agencies have turned their eye to Mars as the next place to explore.

Space agencies like NASA have a long way to go before someone is walking around on Mars, but they have put a human presence on the surface in the form of rovers.

The Mars Rovers are remotely controlled vehicles capable of withstanding the cold temperatures of Mars and sending back vital data to NASA. There have been six rovers launched and operated on Mars, with the first being Sojourner in 1997 and the latest being Perseverance launched in 2021 and is still in operation. In fact, Perseverance is not alone on Mars, with fellow rover Curiosity also on the surface, conducting research.

The vehicles are equipped with sophisticated analytical equipment as well as cameras that provide photographs and video footage of Mars. Through the rovers we've learned about Mars' history, its climate, and whether there may have been microbiological alien life at a time in the far distant past. Exploration at this level involves a great deal of cooperation between the world's scientists, working without borders in the pursuit of knowledge. It's worth it, as there's serious potential behind the Mars missions.

NASA is looking to send people to Mars in the not-so-distant future, after two decades of research from the rovers, and it's important to consider what the implications of that are. Once we've traveled to Mars, are we going to colonize the planet? Are we going to mine minerals that may be valuable to humanity, while living in oxygen-fed tunnels or possibly even underground? Maybe Mars will simply become an outpost, from which space organizations will be able to launch missions that can travel further than they could on Earth.

The possibilities are many regarding Mars, but the ongoing project to travel there has already led to great technological innovation, international cooperation, and the possibility of the first interplanetary colonization. It's a positive sign that we're able to work toward such an ambitious goal - even if we're not quite there yet!

Learning Without Schools

This story will read a little bit like an advert for two websites, and if it makes you visit them, then this book has had a positive impact on your life, so you're welcome.

One of the everlasting debates around education is the cost of it. College and university education can plunge students into vast amounts of debt, sometimes a crippling amount. The textbooks are stupidly expensive, fees can escalate into hundreds of thousands of dollars, and that's without counting rent, food, and everything else that goes with being a student. Basically, it can be pretty expensive.

It's this motivation that drove two people to create excellent education opportunities, at a similar standard to paid courses, that are offered to the world for free. These two people are:

1. Luis von Ahn – the creator of Duolingo
2. Sal Khan – the creator of Khan Academy.

Von Ahn created the company reCAPTCHA, which was sold to Google in 2009. Basically, he's responsible for those "Click this box if you're not a robot" questions you get when you sign up for a new website. Though a little annoying, this technology has helped prevent scammers from using websites to steal our identities and money.

Von Ahn used some of the money earned from this deal to start Duolingo, a website (now best accessed by an app) launched in 2011, which helps you learn a foreign language for free. The company is valued at approximately $1.5 billion. It gains from some advertising revenue but doesn't charge the user. Von Ahn and co-creator Severin Hacker have kept it accessible, and millions of users go on it every day to learn any language from French to Hawaiian to Scottish Gaelic.

Sal Khan's story is different, but his creation is just as helpful to learners. Khan is a businessman, and as a graduate of MIT and Harvard, he's exceptionally smart and was able to earn a decent living from working as a hedge fund analyst in the 2000s. In 2004, he began educating his cousin over the internet. He did it so well that other relatives and friends sought help with mathematics, so Khan moved his lessons onto YouTube for ease of access; by 2009, his videos were so popular on the site that he quit his job!

Khan began working hard on his videos, with sponsorships coming in from donors and advertisers, who enjoyed his videos. The channel grew into the Khan Academy, which to date has received billions of views and interactions. Courses have been designed by specialists, to lead students from the basic knowledge to a very proficient level. It even provides certificates upon completion of the course. Khan Academy helped inspire Coursera, a similar platform with other online courses available.

Essentially, these are stories of free education and its importance. Anyone from anywhere in the world with an internet connection can use sites and apps like Khan Academy, Coursera, and Duolingo to learn coding, mathematics, English literature, and German for free. The work undertaken to do this is incredible and very generous. Both Von Ahn and Khan could certainly charge $10 per course and make themselves hundreds of millions, but they've acknowledged the far greater value of improving people's education for free.

Born to Re-Wild

Most of humanity would likely agree that we've not been the kindest to Mother Nature during our time on Earth. We've spent several thousand years developing, urbanizing, and industrializing, which has led to millions of cities and towns that don't have much of a connection with the natural environment. We're as developed as we've ever been, but there's been a surge in people seeking to put an end to that disconnect. They want to bring their lives back in alignment with nature.

This is a concept called "re-wilding," the scale of which has been staggering. It could be accomplishing something grand in our fight against past and present climate change.

Re-wilding is essentially allowing an area to grow as it naturally would, without interference. This might mean not touching your front garden with a pair of shears or a lawn mower. Over time, weeds will spring up, flowers will bloom, and insects will roam through the garden, as intended. There's something dramatic about it, when compared to the neatly trimmed and preened yards that many of us are accustomed to, but it's really not that shocking. It's just some long grass!

The process takes place on a grander scale as well. For example, since 2006, the Gorongosa National Park in Mozambique has allowed animal populations to grow without interference and has even reintroduced species like the buffalo and zebra. As a result, the ecosystem of the national park has improved dramatically, with biodiversity increasing and healthy population numbers of many animals sustaining themselves. Meanwhile, the Affric Highlands in Scotland started a 30-year-long rewilding project in 2021 that will cover more than 500,000 acres of highland. Trees are protected from logging, flowers remain unpicked, and the grassy fields are allowed to simply grow. The process has already seen a healthier animal population and a promising return in tree numbers.

Re-wilding is currently in vogue and very popular. Cities have begun to permit wild grasses to grow on rooftops, and there's a greater emphasis on allowing nature to exist in and among our urban environments.

Re-wilding isn't going to save the planet on its own, but the initiative is important. In the Western world in particular, we've become increasingly separated and disengaged from our natural world. Concrete jungles have replaced national parks and woodlands, while our hours spent on trains and in cars rob us of the opportunity to simply walk through a field. Re-wilding is supposed to be a re-wilding of humanity, as well as our environment. Allowing ourselves to disconnect from our virtual worlds and protected homes to be around nature more can only benefit our souls.

The projects described here are only the start of the re-wilding process. Small and grand government initiatives will likely spring up as the fight against climate change continues, and we will see more of our world embraced in the bosom of Mother Nature.

The Almighty Donut Boy

If you'd discovered that your nickname was "Donut Boy," you'd be forgiven for perhaps being a little bit sensitive about this, perhaps saying, "I've put on some weight over the last few months, but come on!" For Tyler Carach from Escambia County, Florida, however, it's an honor and a title that he's worked hard to achieve over the last six years.

His campaign to become Donut Boy began innocently enough in 2016 when he visited the store with Sheena, his mother; he was only eight years old at the time. As Tyler and Sheena walked toward the store, Tyler acknowledged that there were four police deputies outside, talking. Tyler turned to his mother and asked, "Can I get them some donuts?" Sheena gave Tyler his pocket money, he purchased a box of sweet pastries, gave them to the deputies, and thanked them for their service as police officers.

Tyler was initially baffled at the deputy's response. They were so grateful for the gift, thanking him again and again. Tyler's innocence protected him from understanding what was truly at play. Police officers all over the world, particularly in America, are under a lot of scrutiny and pressure. In the 2010s, American officers faced accusations of institutional racism, public scandals, and numerous other problems. For the vast majority of diligent, hard-working officers who keep America safe, this can make life difficult. Seeing a child give a small gift and saying thank you can mean the world to those officers.

Tyler is now 15 years old and has dedicated massive amounts of his own spare time to continue his ordained task of delivering donuts to America's police officers. By 2022, he had visited all 50 states and had managed to hand out more than 100,000 donuts directly to police officers. He hasn't managed this by being extremely wealthy; he's worked hard for those "power rings" (Tyler's name for donuts).

Tyler spends a lot of his time writing proposals to companies and asking for donations from local bakeries and donut shops. Dunkin' Donuts sponsored him for a large part of his journey, helping provide thousands of treats for Tyler's distribution. Tyler quickly became a dab hand at public speaking, something which frightens most adults. Appearing on *The Steve Harvey Show*, he had a chance to speak about why he's taken on the strange but dedicated mission. While traveling to Washington D.C., Tyler spoke at a public event with thousands of people in attendance about the good work that police officers do in America.

Tyler created a cape early on in his mission. The cape proudly reads "I DONUT NEED A REASON TO THANK A COP." The teenager still wears it while handing out donuts, though he hasn't stopped at baked goods. During the COVID-19 pandemic, Tyler worked hard, using his connections as Donut Boy to acquire $200,000 worth of hand sanitizer, which he distributed to hospitals, schools, churches, and other places. Tyler's campaigning and partnerships with outdoors companies have helped raise funds to buy smaller police departments new equipment, helping them conduct their jobs.

Tyler's story is a unique one. There aren't many teenagers who'd spend vast amounts of their time donating donuts to police officers. But his story is a bit of a mood-raiser. We're so often divided by our generations, millennial-this and boomer-that. It's important to be reminded that there are kind, thoughtful people everywhere and that today's kids are just as sensitive and thoughtful as young people have ever been.

Vigilante Justice, with Bamboo

In 2006, a superhero group emerged from the dust of violence and abuse. The group continues to stand up for what is correct, fighting against corruption and misdeeds where they see it. We're not talking about the release of *X-Men: The Last Stand*. We're instead talking about the Gulabi Gang, which operates in the Banda District, Uttar Pradesh, in India.

The Gulabi Gang literally means "Pink Gang," a reference to the pink saris that the members wear. The group, which currently has approximately 300,000 members, is entirely made up of women activists who fight for the rights of women across India. Sampat Pal Devi founded the Gulabi Gang. She is a former child bride and mother to five who has witnessed the mistreatment of women in her community all her life. She'd suffered abuse as a child and felt that the standards imposed on women were not necessarily the same for men.

The Gang is a product of its environment, with the Banda District having a particularly poor record of violence toward women. Young women have poor literacy rates and school attendance, and there is a high number of reports of child marriage. The Banda District didn't value the rights of its women and Sampat felt that the influence of unchallenged sexism was too great. So, the Gulabi Gang took to the streets of the district, adorned in pink saris and wielding bamboo sticks as a weapon.

The Gang has been verbally accosted by politicians who were furious about some of their more violent acts, which are strictly employed as a last resort. The Gang uses their sticks to thrash men who are enacting domestic or sexual violence; they first ask the man to stop and, if that fails, they beat him into stopping. The group maintains that this is uncommon, and they're only punishing the men as the police fail to, explaining:

> *"If a woman seeks the membership of Gulabi Gang, it is because she has suffered injustice, has been oppressed and does not see any other recourse. All our women can stand up to the men and if need be, seek retribution through lathis [bamboo sticks]."*

It's generally seen that those who criticize the gang aren't concerned so much about the actual violence of their actions but about the warped traditional gender roles that the Gang threatens. The Gang has pointed out how politicians were happy to criticize their methods, but not so happy to address the serious problems that unchecked aggression toward women brings.

Since 2006, the group has advocated for women. The Gang has organized fundraisers, and through donations has managed to enact great change for women in their community. Their main concern was the low literacy rates, as they felt that uneducated women were unlikely to be able to recognize abuse, nor achieve a good enough position to change things. The group set up a school in 2008, which 800 girls attend. The gang visits families to encourage them to send their female children to school and further education such as university or college, rather than thinking of marriage first.

The Gulabi Gang are fantastic ambassadors for women in a country that has struggled to empower its female population. Traditional gender roles are very much the norm in some areas of India, and women are unfairly subjugated. In the 2020s, there are signs of institutional sexism being slowly dismantled, but there's a long way to go. But the old women smacking a domestic abuser with a large stick while dressed in pink is a powerful image.

$20 to Heal Hearts,
What a Bargain

Money makes the world go around, world go around, the world go around - so goes the famous song from *Cabaret*. Indeed, it does, and it feels that as the world has become more populated and more competitive, we more veraciously chase after the dollar.

We seek money because of what it represents: a new house, a new phone, a car, security, health insurance, and all of the goods that we need to live in the modern world. This means that what we teach children about money is especially important. In an ideal world, they would be able to see that money can be used to feed the soul and provide benefits beyond the superficial.

This brings us to our last story, that of a boy called Jack Swanson, a seven-year-old from Texas who in 2015 was saving for an iPad and had managed to bring his total to $20. He was proud of his figure so far and intended to keep going until he reached the necessary amount for his iPad.

That was until early November when his local community was rocked by a bout of racist vandalism targeting the local mosque, a place of worship for Muslims. Jack sat down with his mother, and they discussed what had happened. Jack said that the offensive acts weren't fair, and the Muslim community didn't deserve to have something precious ruined. He agreed with his mother that the $20 he'd saved so far would be better used as a donation to help the mosque rather than being spent on an iPad.

His donation of $20, of course, doesn't go very far in the adult world. But for Faisal Naeem, a board member of the mosque, the donation meant far more than its financial worth. He said:

> "It's 20 bucks but coming from Jack collecting his pennies it's worth 20 million bucks to me and to our community. This gives me hope because this means it's not one versus the other."

Jack received publicity for his act of kindness, and the donation helped the local community heal. Local and national newspapers reported on the boy with a heart of gold who acknowledged racism when he saw it. Knowing that the hateful act didn't represent the thoughts

187

of the entire neighborhood helped the Muslim community to begin to move on.

Arsalan Iftikhar, who's known on Twitter as The Muslim Guy, read about Jack's generosity and was touched by the gesture. Arsalan is a human rights lawyer and the editor of *The Islamic Monthly Magazine*. As such, he holds a significant reputation, particularly within American Muslim communities. He bought Jack a brand-new iPad as a token of his gratitude. Iftikhar also wrote a letter to Jack thanking him for his kindness and informing Jack that Muslims across the country were grateful.

When we see instances of hate, it's difficult to do the right thing and to stand up for it. Humans have seen enough of what happens when hateful actions aren't challenged and are allowed to flourish, but we can become scared to act, even in the smallest of ways. Jack's small act of generosity did far more work than the racist vandals could ever do. It's heartening to think that our young generation may all be as thoughtful as Jack, and as generous with what little they have. It's a good sign for the future.

CONCLUSION

And so, we stumble into the last few words of this book. If you've made it this far, then hopefully you've enjoyed reading *Positive Stories for the Curious Soul*. The book has been written to entertain and enlighten, as well as to provide a chunk of optimism at a difficult time.

If this book has a point or a message, it's to remain optimistic, thoughtful, and loving even if other people aren't doing so. It's probably time to remind ourselves again of the quote that has driven the purpose of the book:

> *"They say a person needs just three things to truly be happy in this world: someone to love, something to do, and something to hope for."*

If you're very lucky in this world, you'll have all three of these things and will register very highly on the Bhutan GNH index. If you feel as if you're missing some part of this, then remember that it's all achievable, no matter your age. We can love each other without romance. We can find something to do that isn't our work. And we just have to look beyond the scary headlines to see there's plenty to hope for.